helvetica helvetica
helvetica helvetica
helvetica helvetica
helvetica helvetica
helvetica helvetica
helvetica helvetica
helvetica helvetica
helvetica helvetica helvetica
helvetica helvetica helvetica
helvetica helvetica helvetica
helvetica helvetica
helvetica helvetica
helvetica helvetica
helvetica helvetica
helvetica helvetica
helvetica helvetica
helvetica helvetica
helvetica helvetica
helvetica helvetica
helvetica helvetica helvetica helvetica helvetica helvetica
helvetica helvetica helvetica helvetica helvetica helvetica helvetica
helvetica helvetica helvetica helvetica helvetica helvetica
helvetica helvetica helvetica
helvetica helvetica
helvetica helvetica
helvetica helvetica
helvetica helvetica
helvetica helvetica
helvetica helvetica
helvetica helvetica
helvetica helvetica
helvetica helvetica
helvetica helvetica
helvetica helvetica

*Dédicaé aux apprentis
compositeurs typographes de
l'Ecole professionnelle de Porrentruy
en compagnie de leur maître,
M. Chatelain, en souvenir de leur
visite dans nos usines*

*Munchenstein,
le 11 septembre 1968
La direction de la
Fonderie de Caractères Haas S.A.*

To claim that Helvetica has no character is a malicious lie. Ralph Schraivogel

helve
tica

Nouvelle
Antique
Haas

Fonderie
de Caractères
Haas S.A.
Munchenstein
Suisse

A triumph of branding. It wouldn't have been nearly as successful named Neue Haas Grotesk or Germanica.
Henry Steiner

ABCDEFGHI
JKLMNOPQR
STUVWXYZ
ÆŒÇØŞ
1234567890
£$&/!?%

,ˆˇˆˉ°···.,:;-'‚„»›*—

abcdefghijkl
mnopqrstuvw
xyz
æœchckßäáà
âãåçéèêëğ
íìîïijñöóòôõø
şüúùû

Kieler Woche 21.-28. Juni 1964

sfeerbepalende stromingen in de beeldende kunst

nieuw beelden 1965

konstruktivisme   strukturisme   tachisme

ekspressionisme

pop art

vitalisme

figuratisme

unitair urbanisme   realisme

art brut   licht en beweging

stedelijk museum amsterdam 29 mei 20 juni

onder auspicien van de stichting liga nieuw beelden

die gute Form

Kunstgewerbemuseum Zürich

Ausstellung der an der Schweizer Mustermesse Basel ausgezeichneten Gegenstände,
ergänzt mit weiteren Objekten. Veranstaltet vom Schweizerischen Werkbund SWB
21. August bis 3. Oktober 1954
Oeffnungszeiten: Werktags 10-12, 14-18 Uhr, Mittwoch bis 21 Uhr, Samstag und Sonntag
bis 17 Uhr, Montag geschlossen

FONTANA GALLERIA LA POLENA GENOVA 1-28 OTTOBRE 1966

Helvetica – the epitome of ugliness. Wolfgang Weingart

DESIGN: ALAN FLETCHER PENTAGRAM

MARIO BELLINI,
ARCHITECT/DESIGNER
GIVES THE FIRST ANNUAL
PENTAGRAM LECTURE. THE
DESIGN MUSEUM 22 MAY 1991.
WEDNESDAY FROM 7.30 TO 9PM.
TICKETS £10, CONCESSIONS £7.50,
FROM THE DESIGN MUSEUM
BUTLERS WHARF, LONDON
SE1 2YD. TELEPHONE:
071 403 6933 BETWEEN
9.30/5.30 WEEKDAYS,
OR FAX 071 378 6540.
MARIO BELLINI IS
AN ARCHITECT AND
PRODUCT DESIGNER OF
ENORMOUS RANGE AND VARIETY:
THE TOKYO DESIGN CENTRE, A MAJOR
EXPANSION OF THE SITE OF THE MILAN FAIR.
THE CAB CHAIR FOR CASSINA. THE PERSONA AND
FIGURA OFFICE CHAIRS FOR VITRA. THE DIVISUMMA
LOGOS CALCULATORS AND THE ETP 55 TYPEWRITER
FOR OLIVETTI, FOR WHOM HE HAS BEEN CONSULTANT
SINCE 1962. MEMBER OF THE EXECUTIVE COMMITTEE
OF THE MILAN TRIENNALE IN 1986. PLANNED THE HUGE
PROGETTO DOMESTICO EXHIBITION. EDITOR OF DOMUS.
HE HAS WON NUMEROUS AWARDS: THE COMPASSO D'ORO
IN ITALY, THE ANNUAL AWARD IN THE USA, THE MADE IN
GERMANY AWARD, THE GOLD MEDAL IN SPAIN. TWENTY
OF HIS DESIGNS ARE IN THE PERMANENT COLLECTION OF
THE MUSEUM OF MODERN ART IN NEW YORK, WHERE AN
EXHIBITION DEVOTED TO HIS WORK WAS HELD IN 1987.

For me, this typeface does not even exist. Helmut Schmid

musica viva

v
i
v
a

musica viva-konzert

donnerstag, 8. januar 1970
20.15 uhr
grosser tonhallesaal

12. sinfoniekonzert
der
tonhalle-gesellschaft zürich

karten zu fr. 1.- bis fr. 5.-

leitung
charles dutoit

solist
karl engel
klavier

tonhalle-
orchester

tonhallekasse, hug, jecklin, kuoni
filiale carillon schweiz. kreditanstalt

klaus huber

györgy ligeti
igor strawinsky

klaus huber

«tenebrae»
für grosses orchester
1966-67
«atmosphères»
konzert
für klavier, blasinstrumente,
kontrabässe und pauke
«tenebrae»
wiederholung

entwurf j. müller-brockmann / druck bollmann zürich

You don't need a reason to like something. Ed Benguiat

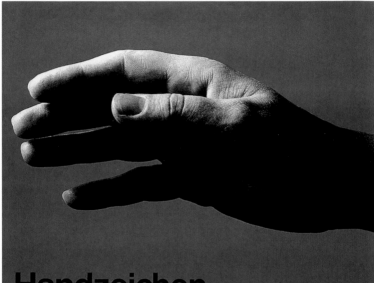

Handzeichen schaffen Klarheit

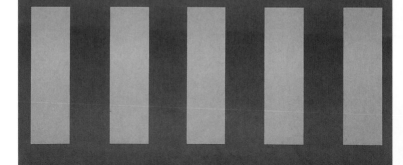

Helvetica communicates with the most legitimate, beautiful, and universal form. Makoto Saito

Preselezione:

Mantenere la direzione

It was easy to become a designer in those days. I looked to mentors like Josef Müller-Brockmann, Paul Rand, Charles Eames, and Helvetica, and found a path of my own. Edgar Reinhard

Wojciech Freudenreich, Poland, 1982

Alkohol niszczy

Unknown, Germany, 1970

Wer trinkt sint k

Barbara Hiestand, Switzerland, 1983

ALKOHOL

16000 Menschen sterben jährlich in der Bundesrepublik an Lungenkrebs.

Vielleicht mal eine weniger...

Von ihnen sind nach der Statistik 99,2 % Raucher, 0,8 % Nichtraucher.

When I studied graphic design between 1967 and 1972, Helvetica was omnipresent. My goal was not to use it.
Niklaus Troxler

Stoppt die Folter.

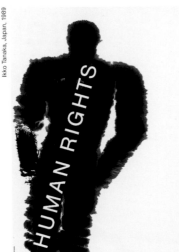

HUMAN RIGHTS

immigration
to
ca nada

1900–75

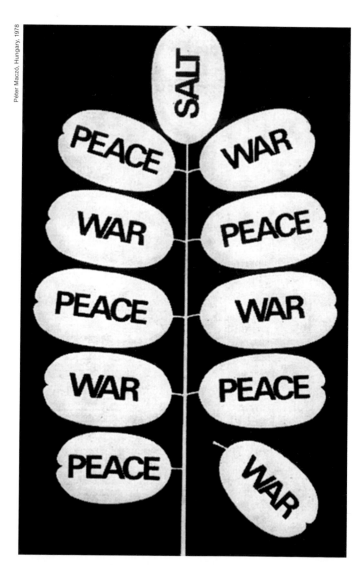

Péter Maczó, Hungary, 1978

Helvetica is the typeface for a deserted island. Friedrich Friedel

Nancy Skolos, Thomas Wedell, USA, 1992

Robert Leydenforst, Don Brewster, USA 1971

Good to the last breath.

Hirokatsu Hijakata, Japan, 1993

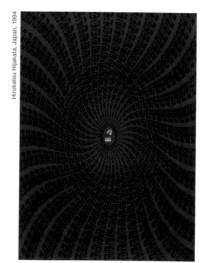

Hirokatsu Hijakata, Japan, 1994

let my people

DAN REISINGER

During the late 1960s and 1970s, Helvetica was not a typeface, it was a lifestyle. Michael Vanderbyl

Roberto, Kuba, 1977

LA JUVENTUD CUBANA
SE SIENTE HEREDERA
DE LA GESTA DE OCTUBRE

Unknown, USA, 1970

L'AMERIQUE LATINE
SERA LE VIETNAM
DEFINITIF
DE L'IMPERIALISME

A AMERICA LATINA
SERA O VIETNAM
DEFINITIVO
DO IMPERIALISMO

CARLOS LAMARCA

LATIN AMERICA
WILL BE
IMPERIALISM'S
DEFINITIVE VIETNAM

Patricio Handl, Austria, 1993

aus
länder

Jacqueline S. Casey, USA

RUSSIA

SE PARLI SOCIALISTA IN
EUROPA TI CAPIRANNO
WENN DU SOZIALISTIS
CH SPRICHST VERSTE
HT MAN DICH IN EURO
PA SI TU PARLES SOCIA
LISTE EN EUROPE ON TE
COMPRENDRA WANNE
ER U SOCIALISTISCH SP
REEKT BEGRIJPT MEN U
IN EUROPA IF YOU SPE
AK SOCIALIST YOU WI
LL BE UNDERSTOOD IN
EUROPE HVIS DU TALER
SOCIALISTISK BLIVER
DU FORSTÅET I EUROPA

PARTITO SOCIALISTA
PSI

la pègre
au
pouvoir

ABOLITION
DE LA
SOCIÉTÉ
DE
CLASSE

CONSEIL POUR LE MAINTIEN DES OCCUPATIONS

Women Now!

Jacquline S. Casey, USA, 1983

AIDS & HERPES

Fact & Fiction

At MIT Compton Gallery lobby
7 days, 9 PM
Events, 8/2D

Sponsored by the
MIT Medical Department
and AIDS
Bring a friend and discuss
the issues that matter to you

Yasumitsu Iguchi, Japan, 1993

Freddie Mercury
s**a**ng songs
Keith Har**i**ng
gave a party in celebration
of his **d**eath one year before
Robert Mapplethorpe
took s**e**lf-portra**i**t**s**
They were always the same
And
what we must not forget
is that lots of p**e**ople
alwa**ys s**upported them
g**e**ntly

Seiler DDB/CR Werbeagentur, Basel, Switzerland, 1995

THE POWER OF LOVE STOP AIDS

A prevention
campaign of the
Swiss Federal
Office of Public
Health in cooperation
with the Swiss
Aids Foundation.

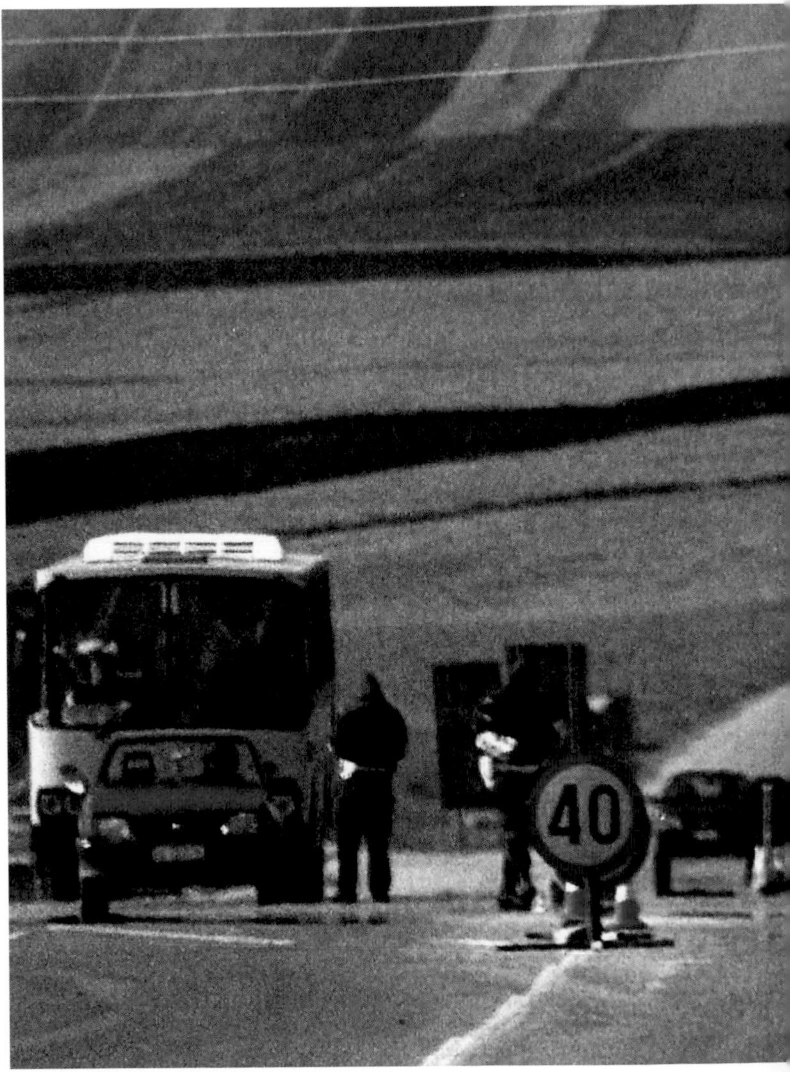

UNHCR

DSB
Danske Statsbaner

⊕ SBB CFF FFS

Settore

C

Automate

```
2  1
```

							Gleis	Hinweis
Abfahrt Départ Partenza								
12.02	EuroCity *EC*	Basel	Karlsruhe	Mannheim	Frankfurt		7	ca. 20 Min. später
12.04	InterCity *IC*	Zürich	Flughafen ✈	Winterthur Wil	St. Gallen		8	
12.06	Schnellzug	Oensingen	Solothurn Biel	Lausanne Sion	Brig		5	
12.15	Regionalzug 👁	Aarburg-Oftringen	Zofingen Sursee		Luzern		4	
12.17	Regionalzug	Aarburg-Oftringen	Langenthal	Burgdorf	Bern		6	Sektor A B
12.18	S1	Tecknau	Liestal		Basel		5	
12.25	Schnellzug	Aarau Brugg	Baden Zürich	Flughafen ✈	St. Gallen		3	

```
12.24 REGIONALZUG NACH BADEN
ABFAHRT MIT BUS AB BAHNHOFPLATZ
```

Gleis

1

r = ½ Grundeinheit

AmericanAirlines®

Lufthansa

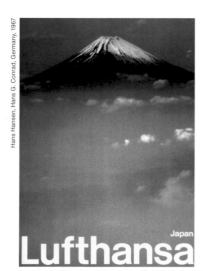

Japan

Lufthansa

España

Lufthansa

Anyone who uses Helvetica knows nothing about typefaces. Wolfgang Weingart

Knoll

Helvetica: Quite frankly, I never liked it that much—too homogenized, too pretty... Univers and Akzidenz Grotesk both have more character. Helvetica cannot be equated with Swiss Design. Swiss Design always stood and still stands for humanistic, clear-cut communication. Fritz Gottschalk

Chermayeff & Geismar, USA, 1993, Corporate Identity

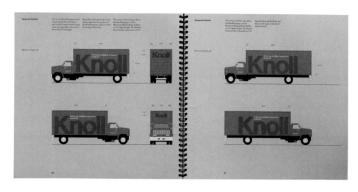

3M

American Airlines

Aer Lingus ☘

ARCO ◆

BayBanks®

BASF

aero**mexico**

A&S

BancOhio
National Bank

Aero**sweet**
AIRLINES

ARMOR ALL

BANK ONE®

AGFA

AT&T
Communications

Bayer

AlliedSignal

ASKO

BDF ●●●●
Beiersdorf

aprilia

auping

Bogner

AVC◆RP

bergamin

AMERICAN
CONTINENTAL
CORPORATION

azs

B&G

Amtrak

AVIACO

Bikuben

Agip

asc

British Gas
E&P

alta**vista:**

Bank of America

BOMBARDIER
AEROSPACE

● **BLAUPUNKT**

Chicks on Speed

bilde&lyd

colette
styledesignartfood

clearNET

◆ Dresdner Bank
Die Beraterbank

*BELL*SOUTH

Coloplast

DSB
Danske Statsbaner

BLESS

COMME des GARÇONS
*

DUCATI

Ⓐ **Bell Atlantic**

BRIGGS & STRATTON

CONAIR

Eagle

■ canvas

COMMUNAUTÉ
URBAINE
DE MONTRÉAL

Eas**Tex**

Cassina

Currys

EVEREX

cappellini

Curtis
Mathes

cable

CUSHMAN&
WAKEFIELD

ЭРКОН◉ПРОДУКТ

Cessna

Def**J**am
recordings

EMI
AMERICA

CATERPILLAR®

ESKOM

east west

 EPA

evian.

FENDI

GM

GG

GREYHOUND

GIRO

Georgia·Pacific

Handelsbanken

Hanes

Hapag-Lloyd

Health o meter ®

Hayes

HOMELITE

HOOVER

HARLEY-DAVIDSON

Humana Hospital

Husqvarna

 **ICRC**

intel ®

IIPPRRAA

JCPenney

Jeep

JOCKEY.

Knoll

Kappa

Kartell

Kawasaki

Kimberly-Clark

LAGERFELD

Leitner_

LASALLE Bank

Letraset®

 **Lufthansa**

Magic Chef®

**MANPOWER**®
TEMPORARY SERVICES

Martin

MATTEL

**MERCURY
OUTBOARDS**

 **MetLife**®

MIGROS

**MILITARY
RELOCATION
NETWORK**

MINDS**E**T

 MOTOROLA

 Miracle-Ear®

**MONEY
SUPPLY**

MOROSO

無印良品
MUJI

Museum Mile

ЯƎZИAИ **NANZER**

NRS

 National®

**NATIONWIDE
INSURANCE**

NAVISTAR SM

N**EE**D

Norelco

Nestlē®

 The New England
Your Financial Partner

northAmerican®
VAN LINES / AGENT

**THE
NORTH
FACE**

 Northeast Savings

NYCE

NYNEX®

Oral-B®

OLYMPUS®

OLYMPIA

**ORCHESTRE
DE CHAMBÉRY
ET DE LA SAVOIE**

ouest
france

 **Pan Am**

Panasonic.

ROYAL

 SEARS

 Paradigm

 The Royal Bank of Scotland

SEARS SAVINGS BANK

Payne

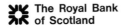 **STIMOROL**

SECURITAS

 Philippine Airlines

 **SAAB**

SE**CŪ**RITY

parmalat

 SEAT

 Pitney Bowes

salton

SERVI★TAR.

Pollenex.

 **SAMSUNG** ELECTRONICS

SHEAFFER.

P DR

Signal

 Pressman®

 SANDVIK Rock Tools

S I S L E Y

Proctor+Silex.

 SBB CFF FFS

 ŠKODA AUTO

 **ПрограмБанк**

 scitex

 smeg tecnologia che arreda

The **Prudential**

SANYO

SOHIO

 **PubliSer**

SCP

 Southern States

STAPLES

STAR BANK

STARCRAFT

SUN

Sun Bank

Swimaster

TANDEM

TRANS WORLD EXPRESS **TW EXPRESS**

TARGET

TEXACO

Thaibook

TISSOT

totes

TOYOTA

 *ТРАНСАЭРО* АВИАЛИНИИ

Tupperware®

TYROLIA

UNIFOR

UNION CARBIDE

United Banks of Colorado, Inc.

UNITED UNITED UNITED Van Lines

Toastmaster

UNITED TECHNOLOGIES CHEMICAL SYSTEMS

USLIFE

U.S. MAIL

USX

V2

V·A·G

WESTERN DIGITAL

xanax

YORX

YORK® Heating and Air Conditioning

ZANUSSI

ZedzzZ

McCann-Erickson S.A., Switzerland, 1997

Warum gibt es hier noch freie Parkplätze?

⟨↔⟩ SBB

Publicis, Switzerland, 2002

FRO AGE

M EST À L'EXPO.02

Orange, 2001

Here too

Best reception.
Highest sound quality.

The future's bright. The future's Orange.

Wer sorgt im Schnellzugtempo für gutes Klima?

Klimatisierte InterRegio statt Schnellzüge.

SBB

PO   ODORI

M È ALL'EXPO.02

Ici comme
ailleurs

Meilleure réception.
Meilleure qualité sonore.

The future's bright. The future's Orange.

Marc Atlan, France, 1994–1998

Helvetica is the jeans, and Univers the dinner jacket. Helvetica is here to stay. Adrian Frutiger

october 13th - november 6th .mark borthwick synthetic notes
october 13th self service images 120x160

colette

colette
styledesignartfood

colette

COLETTE N°3
LOUIE AUSTEN: MUSIC
BERTRAND BURGALAT &
A.S DRAGON: FOLLOW ME
FAT TRUCKERS: SUPERBIKE
CROSSOVER: EXTENSIVE CARE
ANDRE POPP: BALLADE A LA ROSE
SLY, LENKY & FRENCHIE: DARKSIDE
NOVOTONES: PORQUE TE VAS
TUXEDOMOON & HELL: LUTHER BLISSET
CHICKS ON SPEED: FASHION RULES
PEACHES: SET IT OFF
MOCKY: SWEET MUSIC
THE NOTWIST: PILOT VITALIC: PONEY PT.1
JAPANESE TELECOM: PAGODA OF SIN

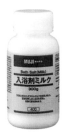
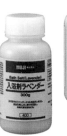

tribeca ISSEY MIYAKE: A Collaborative Space Opening September 2001 Continuing work-in-progress: Issey Miyake, Frank Gehry, Naoki Takizawa, Gordon Kipping, Makiko Minagawa, Dai Fujiwara, Neville Brody, Alexandre Gehry and others to come.

tribeca

ISSEY MIYAKE

119 Hudson Street, New York T: 212 226 0100 tribeca@isseymiyake.com www.isseymiyake.com

If you have no intuitive sense of design, then call yourself an 'information architect' and only use helvetica.
David Carson

tribeca
isseymiyake
sale
springsummer
2002 starts
thursday
june 13

THING YOU NEED. YOU COME TO ME, I'M YOUR MAN. AND STEVEN WILL YOU KNOW, I ALWAYS WANTED TO KNOW, STEVEN, OF ALL THE THINGS THAT YOU COULD ASK FOR, WHY WOULD YOU ASK FOR THAT? YOU KNOW THAT STANLEY DOESN'T TAKE MEETINGS. "WELL, YOU SAID THAT IF THERE WAS ANYTHING I WANTED." GABRIEL SAYS: "I'M REALLY SORRY, I CAN'T DO THAT." SO NOW HE'S SHOWING HIM AROUND HEAVEN AND STEVEN SEES THIS GUY WEARING AN ARMY JACKET WITH A BEARD RIDING A BICYCLE AND STEVEN SAYS TO GABRIEL: "OH MY GOD, LOOK, OVER THERE THAT'S STANLEY KUBRICK, COULDN'T WE JUST STOP HIM AND SEE HE'S AND GABRIEL PULLS STEVEN TO THE SIDE AND SAYS: "THAT'S NOT STANLEY KUBRICK, THAT'S GOD - HE JUST THINKS HE'S STANLEY KUBRICK."

Ferdinand Kriwet, Germany, 1975

Kazuyo Sejima, Japan, 1993

Signo, Italy, 1968

Rr
oo
aa

12

I remember a time at Yale when my work was being critiqued by Paul Rand. Mr. Rand told me only to use Helvetica as a display face, never in text. Then he squinted, leaned in, and whispered in my ear, "because Helvetica looks like dogshit in text" Kyle Cooper

r r r
a r
r a a
a r r r

Rrrrooooaaarrrrr!

The perfection of Helvetica is its letterspacing capabilities – it leads to perfection in shape and form, but like a beautiful person it often lacks personality. Keith Godard

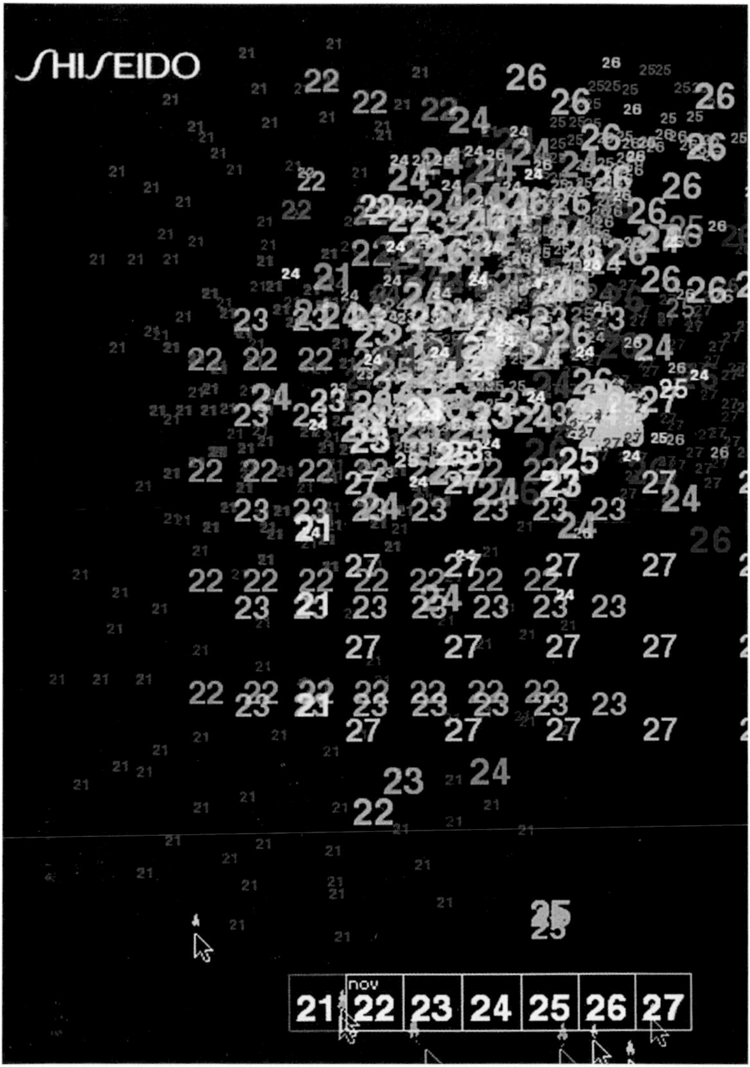

John Maeda, USA, 1997

Frieder Grindler, Germany, 1966

Walter Ballmer, Italy, 1973

Gianni Bortolotti, Italy, 1984

Max Kisman, The Netherlands, 1987

多彩な食卓　HOUSEFOOD
LOBSTERCOCKTAIL
PATEMOULECANAPE
TERRINESANDWICH
SOUFFLECONSOMME
CREAMSOUPGRATIN
OMELETCROQUETTE
CUTLETBEEFSTEAK
BEEFSTEWCHOWDER
ROASTBEEFPOTATO
EGGHAMBURGSTEAK
CURRY&RICEPILAF
PORKSAUTESHRIMP
SALADHASHEDBEEF
HAMFRIEDCHICKEN
MEATPIEMACARONI
SPAGHETTITOMATO
PIZZARISOTTOVIN
BREADTOASTCREPE
ICECREAMPUDDING
JELLYCOFFEE

ｈ ハウス食品

Helvetica is a reliable and irresistible typeface; it keeps me from being lazy and trying to use other fonts to make my work different. Kan Tai-keung

Scott A. Mednick, USA, 1979

John Melin, Sweden, 1972

Wolfgang Schmidt, Germany, 1963

Signo, Italy, 1975

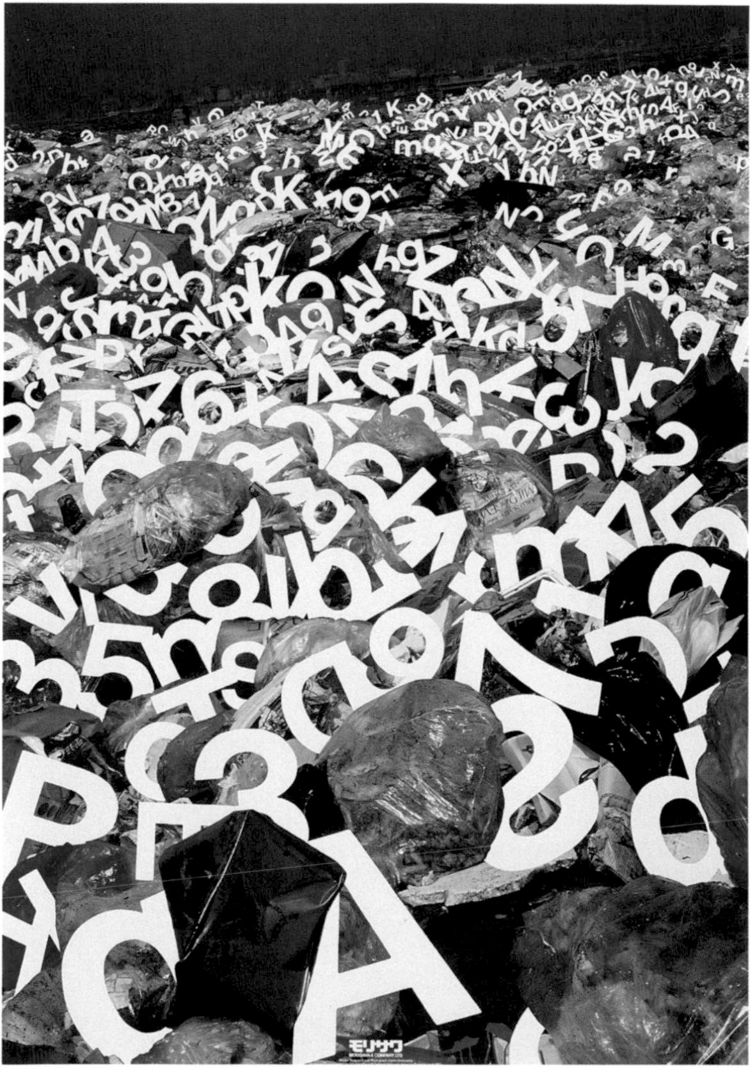

Tauguya Inoue, Japan, 1993

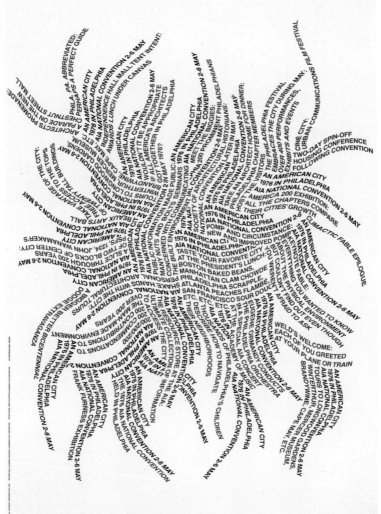

Making a statement with an expressive typeface takes more courage and craftsmanship than taking the apathetic path of least resistance with Helvetica. Erik Spiekermann (from "Ursache und Wirkung")

LA NOUVELLE MUSEE D'ART
FIGURATION ET D'HISTOIRE
AMERICAINE GENEVE
1.2.7-14.9 1969 RAFFAEL GILL
HIGGINS JOHNSON HARRIS
GALLO DIEBENKORN SEGAL
NELSON WARHOL HANSEN
RAUSCHENBERG CREMEAN
BOYCE BATTENBERG JONES
WESSELMANN

Entrèe bd Jaques-Dalcroze

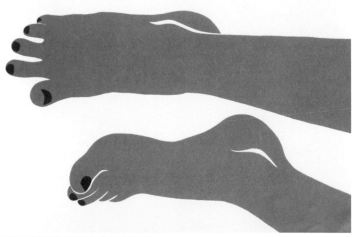

Helvetica. The cream on the pie. Fernando Medina

Helvetica – never liked it, never used it. Willi Kunz

The Helvetica Medium lower case "a" in the original foundry and linotype is the most beautiful two-dimensional form ever designed. Its luxurious sensual curves are balanced by points of crisp tension. Its lovely counter makes me think of Mozart. Its subtlety and complexity make it one of the most difficult forms to draw free-hand. I loved Helvetica in college in 1965; I loved it through our typographic rebellions in 1975, through our vernacular celebrations in 1985, through our post-structuralist resistance to beauty in 1990; and I still love it today. Katherine McCoy

Fotowerke

Balthasar Burkhard

Philip Guston

(1913–1980) Spätwerk

8.5.– 19.6.1983

Kunsthalle
Basel

Täglich durchgehend von 10–17 Uhr, Mittwochabend bei
freiem Eintritt und Führung von 19.30–21.30 Uhr.
Pfingstsonntag geschlossen

Francesco Clemente

Jenny Holzer

Barbara Kruger

13.5.– 24.6.1984

Kunsthalle
Basel

Täglich durchgehend von 10–17 Uhr, Mittwochabend bei
freiem Eintritt und Führung von 19.30–21.30 Uhr.

Malcolm Morley

David Hockney

Fotos von 1962–1982

23.1.– 27.2.1983

Kunsthalle
Basel

Täglich durchgehend von 10–17 Uhr, Mittwochabend bei
freiem Eintritt und Führung von 19.30–21.30 Uhr.

Weihnachtsausstellung

der Basler Künstler und Künstlerinnen

28.11.1982 – 2.1.1983

Kunsthalle Basel
und Kaserne

Täglich durchgehend von 10–17 Uhr. Kunsthalle: Mittwochabend bei freiem
Eintritt und Führung von 19.30–21.30 Uhr. Kaserne: Donnerstagabend
bei freiem Eintritt und Führung von 19.30–21.30 Uhr.
Geschlossen: 24. u. 31.12.82 von 12–17 Uhr. 25.12.82 u. 1.1.83 ganzer Tag

I discovered that I never really used Helvetica but I like to look at it. I like the VW beetle, too, although I've never driven one. Stefan Sagmeister

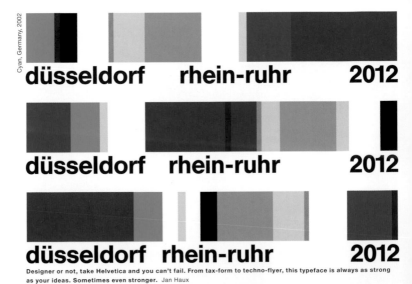

Designer or not, take Helvetica and you can't fail. From tax-form to techno-flyer, this typeface is always as strong as your ideas. Sometimes even stronger. Jan Haux

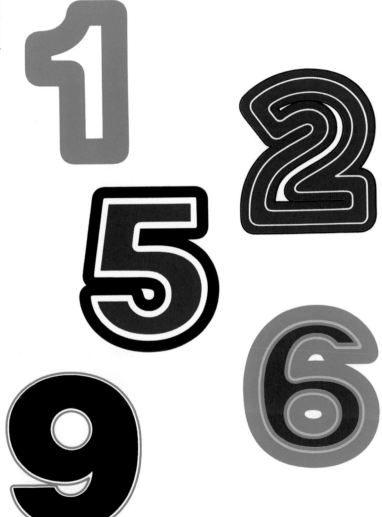

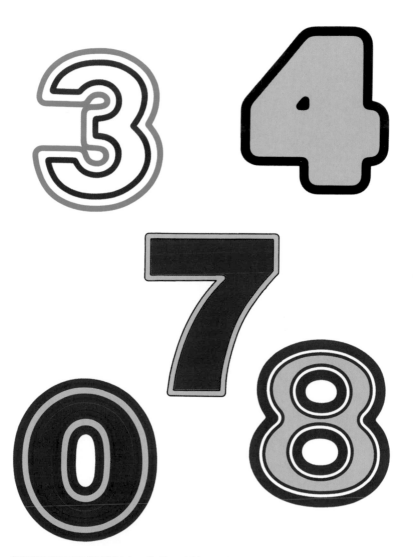

At the very moment we thought it belonged to the past, it became hip again. Finn Skodt

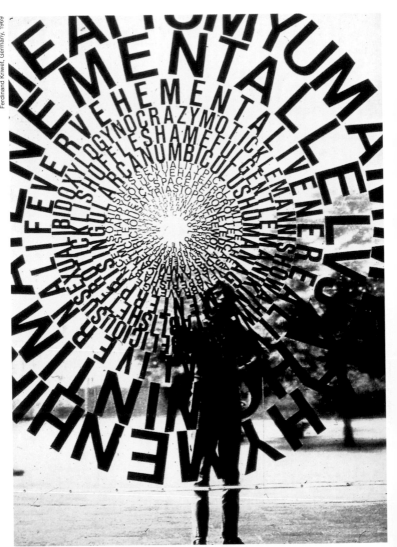

It's like a memory of soil. Mitsuo Katsui

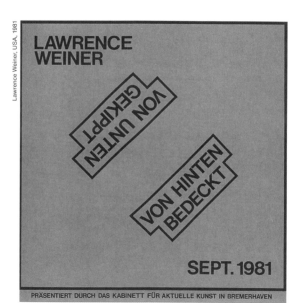

LAWRENCE
WEINER

VON UNTEN
GEKIPPT

VON HINTEN
BEDECKT

SEPT. 1981

PRÄSENTIERT DURCH DAS KABINETT FÜR AKTUELLE KUNST IN BREMERHAVEN

es ist kein schlechter traum
in dem die geschlagenen
nicht zu schlägern werden /
veränderbar ist / wie licht und
schatten fallen / die einsicht /
daß noch nicht gewesen ist / daß
sie nicht stillsteht / sondern
sich dreht / noch ist nicht
aller tage abend / also träume
deinem traum / wandere weiter

Konkrete Jochen Stankowski
Poesie   Peter Grohmann

Richard Prince, "What can you do?", 2001, acrylic on canvas, 191 × 295 cm

Richard Prince, "Paint the Paint", 2001–02, acrylic on canvas, 284 × 508 cm

(Courtesy Barbara Gladstone)

Damien 5036-23

Steak and Kidney*
Ethambutol Hydrochloride

Tablets
400mg

100 Tablets   PIE

Cornish 100mg/5ml
Pasty
Rifampicin B.P.

To be taken by mouth

Peas   CHIPS

100ml Syrup

Chicken®

**Concentrated Oral Solution
Morphine Sulphate**

20mg/ml

**Each 1ml contains Morphine
Sulphate BP 20mg**

120ml

**Damien
Hirst**

30 Tablets

Meatballs

Hirst

150mg

Each film-coated tablet contains
150mg moclobemide

Use only as directed by a physician

KEEP OUT OF REACH
OF CHILDREN

Store in a dry place

GRAVY

PL0031/0275   PA 50/81/2

Hirst Products Limited
Welwyn Garden City England

(Damien Hirst, Booth Clibborn Editions, 2001)

LIONFISH
60c AUSTRALIA

U.S. POSTAGE 8c

AMERICAN
REVOLUTION
BICENTENNIAL
1776-1976

XI. PARTEITAG der SED
10 DDR

USAirmail
31c

VENTESIMO ANNIVERSARIO DELLA REPUBBLICA
1946-2 GIUGNO 1966
L.90 POSTE ITALIANE

5 भारत INDIA

SANTIER
1°⁰
POSTA ROMANA

ESCUELA MILITAR
1885-25 DE AGOSTO-1985
100 AÑOS FUNDACION
URUGUAY CORREOS N$10
IMP. NAL 85

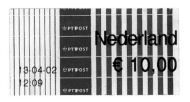

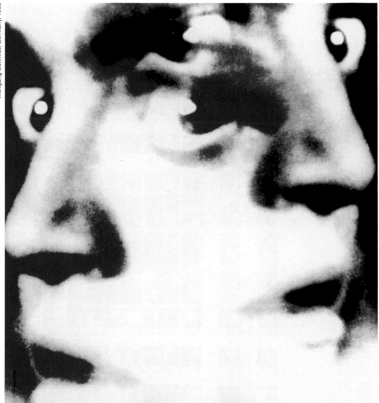

Peter Lorre
Gustaf Gründgens
Theo Lingen
Otto Wernicke
in Fritz Langs

Ein Atlas Film

M

Eine Stadt
jagt einen Mörder

Das unübertroffene
Meisterwerk
des deutschen
Kriminalfilms

Prädikat:
Besonders wertvoll

EIN WAHRHAFT GROSSER FILM

URTEIL VON NÜRNBERG

Stanley Kramer zeigt

Spencer
Tracy

Burt
Lancaster

Richard
Widmark

Marlene
Dietrich

Maximilian
Schell

Judy
Garland

Montgomery
Clift

als Irene Hoffman

UNITED
ARTISTS

Prod. und Regie
Stanley Kramer

P. BOUVIER   AFFICHES ATAR, GENÈVE

Choose Life. Choose a job. Choose a career. Choose a family. Choose a fucking big television, choose washing machines, cars, compact disc players and electrical tin openers. Choose good health, low cholesterol, and dental insurance. Choose fixed interest mortgage repayments. Choose a starter home. Choose your friends. Choose leisurewear and matching luggage. Choose a three-piece suite on hire purchase in a range of fucking fabrics. Choose DIY and wondering who the fuck you are on a Sunday morning. Choose sitting on that couch watching mind-numbing, spirit-crushing game shows, stuffing fucking junk food into your mouth. Choose rotting away at the end of it all, pishing your last in a miserable home, nothing more than an embarrassment to the selfish, fucked up brats you spawned to replace yourself.

Choose your future.
Choose life.

Trainspotting

BRAD PITT   MORGAN FREEMAN

Helvetica is like a diamond. It must be handled with care – cut to reveal its beauty and polished to make it shine.
Otherwise, it is ordinary, like any other stone. Philippe Apeloig

Base, Belgium, 2002

Vidar Hekkelstrand, Sweden, 2001

Fernando Gutiérrez, Spain, 1998

Exquisite Corporation, USA, 2001

Robert Hales, USA, 1996

Yorgo Tloupas, United Kingdom, 2002

Switzerland, 1998

Nicolas Zentner, Switzerland, 2002

Margherita La Noce & Filippo Mazzocchi, Italy, 2002

Years ago when Haber still set all type for Bazaar I was approached to do a type book for Haber. Helvetica was one of the fonts I agreed to do. I still think it is one of

Tomás Gonda, Germany, 1962

Work in Progress, France, 2002

Christoph Rauch, Attila Menesi, Germany, 1999

Mario Romano, Switzerland, 2002

Stephen Male, United Kingdom, 2000

Experimental Jetset, The Netherlands, 2001

Amelia Pema, Italy, 2000

Stephen Gan, USA, 1996

Patrick van Dam, The Netherlands, 2002

1960 wow / 1970 ok / 1980 boring / 1990 dead / 2000 cool Mervyn Kurlansky

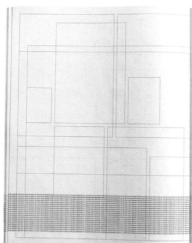

Q: How many Emigre products does it take to change a lightbulb?

Magneto Optical Disc ■ Ez Flyer ■ Paper Punch Card ▨ Travan ■ Tel Dec ■ Floppy Disk ■ Phonovision ● Capacitance Elec tronic Disc ■ Neo Geo ■ Video Long Player ● TelCan ■

8 Track ■ Compac t Disc ● Super Disk ■ 12' Vinyl Record ● Viewmaster ◉ Video 2000 ■ Digi tal Versatile Disc R am ■ Syquest ■ U matic ■ Play tape ■ Compact Flash Card ■ Dec Tape ●

It's like running into an old girl friend and being surprised at how attractive and sophisticated she still is.
Tobias Keller

Integral Lars Müller, Switzerland, 1999

Sweden, Sweden, 2001

Paul Rand, USA, 1985

Out of the shelves, 2002

Helvetica just plain works. Scott Santoro

Seit seinen analytischen Forschungen über die Ressourcenverteilung auf der Erde in den dreissiger Jahren erstellt Fuller am Entwurf einer Weltkarte, die sich zur Veranschaulichung von globalen Daten und Verhältnissen eignet. Zu Beginn des Weltkrieges bemerkt er eine gefährliche Kluft zwischen dem konventionellen Weltbild und einer Realität, die durch Luftfahrt und -Blitzkriege geprägt ist. Er will die mentale Karte korrigieren, die sich im 400jährigen Gebrauch der Mercator-Projektion in den Köpfen verdichtet hat. Die Dymaxion-Projektion soll den Schlüssel zu absoluter Logistik aus dem Globus liefern. Als topologische Datenübertragung von der Kugel auf die Flächen liefern ein Grossrechensystem war sie für Fuller ein Hilfswerk, die fundamental wichtige Umsteigestation zur integralen synergetischen Geometrie und zu den geodätischen Kuppeln.

DYMAXION
WORLD MAP

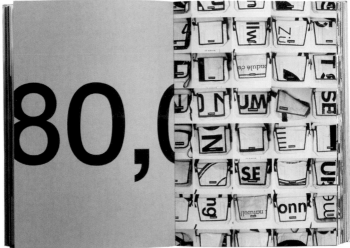

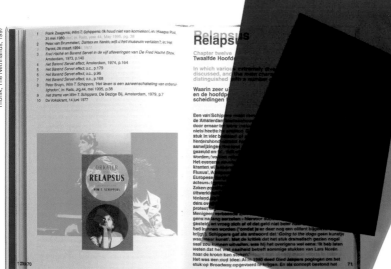

complete weekend paper with the Editor, the Guide, Travel and all the best jobs

The Guardian

Caryl Phillips
The trouble with Leeds United
Weekend

Vic Reeves
Painting, not laughing
Weekend

AC Grayling
The absurd theories of Sigmund Freud
Review

Tom Stoppard
Life behind the camouflage
Review

This time we wasn't robbed

Emma Brockes

In the moments before kick-off, England fans asked themselves the question: "Who are we? Who are we?" Whoever us? Whoever us?

The chant, sung by 4,000 people in Trafalgar Square, was easy to answer. "Were England 'til we die" it rumoured confusingly throughout the 90 minutes, although the nature of the reply became progressively less palatable.

At the final whistle, those who still had the heart to sing, responded in a battle chorus of "Who are ya", with, "Victor-ia, and we know we ate". England had lost, yes, but a fleeting insight that few others had was a dying that, they know it, no deal with.

England captain David Beckham consoles goalkeeper David Seaman over his crucial error Photograph: Dan Chung/Reuters

'I just want to say sorry' – Seaman

Michael Walker in Shizuoka

Castlereagh break-in an 'inside job'

Rosie Cowan, Richard Norton-Taylor and Nick Hopkins

NOT FOR THE FAINT HEARTED

Hürriyet

Türkiye Türklerindir

27 Haziran 2002 Perşembe   Kurucusu: Sedat Simavi 1896-1953

SİZİNLE GURUR DUYUYORUZ

Yarı finale çıktınız. Dünyayı hayran bıraktınız. Bizleri mutlu ettiniz. Türkiye sizinle gurur duyuyor.

4 güçlü ülkeden biriyiz
■ Devlerin elendiği Dünya Futbol Şampiyonası'nda Türkiye'yi dünyanın en güçlü 4 ülkesi arasına sokan sizlere teşekkür ediyoruz. Tüm dünyada günlerdir ay yıldızı konuşturan sizlere teşekkür ediyoruz.

Başa baş oyun, pis bir gol
■ 6 Dünya Kupası'nda final oynamış, dördünde şampiyon olmuş yıldızlar takımı Brezilya, dün başa baş bir oyunla bizi sadakat yenince inanılmaz sevindi. Pis bir gol, Brezilya'yı finale taşıdı. ■ Spor

İşte o talihsiz golle gelen gözyaşları. Bu gözyaşları, Dünya Kupası finalini kaçırdığınız için. Düşünebiliyor musunuz?

Şimdi hedef üçüncülük
■ Senol Güneş'in ve Türkiye'nin aslanları finali kaçırdı ama gururumuzla çalt kırdı. Ayakta alkışlandı. Şimdi 29 Haziran Cumartesi günü Güney Kore'yi devirmeye ve dünya üçüncüsü olmaya çalışacak. ■ Spor'da

Öteki maç sürüyor...

MAÇ bitsam... Hepimiz heyecanların başına takıldı. Brezilya'ya karşı oynayan şampiyonun büyük bir heyecanla ve coşkuyla izledi. Ünsar -futbolun anlam-ların değerlendirmesine gözlerinden işaret fazlasıyla yaşıyor. Ama 4 kere dünya şampiyonu olmuş, altı kere final oynamış bir takıma karşı ne kadar başarı sürdürebilirse o kadar ortaya koyduk. ■ 11'de

Bizi dünya alkışlıyor

BBC: Türkiye'ye atkışlar

■ Türkler, turnuvanın Brezilyadan korkmayan tek takımıydı. Çok iyi mücadele ettiler. Bize çok kaldılı her yarı final izlettiler. Bu maç süper kısa.

Yunan basını: Bravo

■ Türkiye boyun eğmedi. Türkler futbolda devasa adımlar attıklarına kanıtladılar. Brezilya, Türkiye denilen büyük engeli aşmakta zorlandı.

Alman ZDF: Muhteşem

■ Türkler muhteşem bir eşsiz oynadı, ancak son yarım dakik kulü. Türkler milli takımlarıyla gurur duyabilir. Brezilya, Rüştü'ye çok takıldı. ■ Spor

Ankara durunca işler bozuldu

■ Dolar 1 milyon 635 binle 2002'nin ikiz ve yerisine çıktı, borsa dibe oturdu. Standart and Poor's, Türkiye'nin görünümünü, 'pozitif'ten 'duran'a çevirdi. ISO, hükümete karşı deklarasyon hazırladı. Cengiz Sıklakoğlu, "Hükümet sorunu halledilmeden Meclis'in tatile çıkması toplumsal kutlamalar" diye konuştu. ■ Yazısı 13. sayfada

MICHAEL BUTLER PRESENTS

HAIR

THE AMERICAN TRIBAL LOVE ROCK MUSICAL

BOOK & LYRICS: GEROME RAGNI, JAMES RADO/MUSIC: GALT MAC DERMOT
EXECUTIVE PRODUCER: BERTRAND CASTELLI/DIRECTED BY: TOM O'HORGAN

The capital R is the only part of Helvetica that disturbs me. The odd bell-bottom curve of the leg reminds me of that photograph by Robert Mapplethorpe of a guy in a three-piece suit suit with his pants unzipped, exposing this huge, curving penis. The R is both the penis and the three-piece suit all at once. Abbott Miller

Jean-Paul Gorde, France, 1985

France, 2001

Tom Hingston, United Kingdom, 1998

Tibor Kalman, USA, 1980

Jason Claiborne, USA, 1965

Intro, United Kingdom, 1999

8vo, United Kingdom, 1991

Brian Cannon, United Kingdom, 1995

Richard Hamilton, United Kingdom, 1968

The BEATLES

Pentagram, United Kingdom, 1993

Barbara Wojirsch, 1989

RX, United Kingdom, 1983

Vincent Becchinelli, USA, 1995

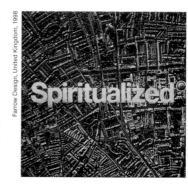

Farrow Design, United Kingdom, 1998

B & B Wojirsch, 1974

David Coleman, USA, 1987

Howard Wakefield, United Kingdom, 1997

Kent Nyberg, Sweden, 1995

In a way, The Beatles are the Helvetica of pop; just like Helvetica is The Beatles of typefaces. Experimental Jetset

Sonic Youth, Christophe Habib, USA, 1997

SONIC YOUTH
ANAGRAMA
IMPROVISATION AJOUTÉE
TREMENS
MIEUX DE CORROSION

SYR
1 STEREO

PERSPECTIVES MUSICALES

Robert Del Naja, Michael Nash, United Kingdom, 1991

massive
attack

Jane Gulick, USA, 1987

LEMONHEADS

HATE YOUR FRIENDS

Pentagram, United Kingdom, 1993

France, 2002

REMIXES

Tom Hingston, United Kingdom, 1999

robbie williams

millennium

Elektrosmog Hindermann+Walser, Switzerland, 2001, Helvetica-Rectangular

! " # $ % & ' ( ) × + , . ∕ 0 1 2
3 4 5 6 7 8 9 : ; ‹ = › ? @ A B
C D E F G H I J K L M N O P Q
R S T U V W X Y Z Ä Ç É N Ö Ü
a b c d e f g h i j k l m n o p q
r s t u v w x y z á à â ä a a ç
é è ê ë í ì î n ó ò ô ö o ú ù û ü
! " # $ % & ' ( ) × + , . ∕ 0 1 2 3 4 5 6 7 8 9 : ;
‹ = › ? @ A B C D E F G H I J K L M N O P Q R
S T U V W X Y Z Ä Ç É N Ö Ü a b c d e f g
h i j k l m n o p q r s t u v w x y z á à â ä a ç
é è ê ë í ì î n ó ò ô ö o ú ù û ü

Elektrosmog Hindermann+Walser, Pierre Miedinger, Switzerland, 2001, Brauer-Regular

0123456789{%¡;&?

ABCDEFGHIJKLMNOP

QRSTUVWXYZ†~}«<#Nº

abcdefghijklmnopqrstu

vwxyz[¶]$£¢¥€>ÿŸ°§÷

Æªfifl@.–(ÅØßœõîé)

It amazes me how many people have an opinion about Helvetica who couldn't pick it out of a type lineup if their reputation depended on it. Douglas Wadden

ABCDEFGHIJKLMNOP

QRSTUVWXYZ ÄÖÜ

ÀÂÁÈÊÉÌÎÍÒÔÓÙÛÚ

abcdefghijklmnopqrs

tuvwxyz äöü

àâáèêéìîíòôóùûú

1234567890£$&/!?%

.,:;-.. ''‚'"" «+» *

{}[]()†#ⒶⒷⒸⒹ™=

Helvetica is like a good screwdriver; a reliable, efficient, easy-to-use tool. But put it in the wrong hands and it's potentially lethal. Tom Geismar

8vo, United Kingdom, 1989

Bark, United Kingdom, 2002

Sex without love. Its lack of volition is pure denial. You can do whatever you want with it. It doesn't resist or agree.
It is still water with a smooth surface, perfectly mirroring the lover of the moment. Clemens Schedler

Helvetica is to typeface as Toblerone is to chocolate. Alan Fletcher

FANSHOPPING®

WWW.FANCLUBNETWORK.COM

GIRLS 3 STAGE T-SHIRT
SLEEVE: SHORT/CAP/VEST
NECK: ROUND/V NECK
HEM: STRAIGHT/CURVED

ENGINEERED
JEANS™

FREITAG

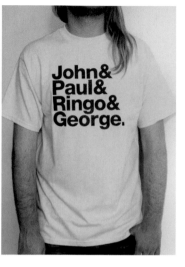

Experimental Jetset, The Netherlands, 2001

Maureen Mooren, Daniel van der Velden, The Ntetherlands, 1998

Stella McCartney, France, 2002

Jack Summerford, USA, 1989

Helvetica to me is a bit like pasta. Basta. Cornel Windlin

Any good typeface can be completely destroyed when misused or extensively overused. Helvetica seemed to sustain a beating like no other. Still fresh, still popular: Helvetica is king! Alexander Gelman

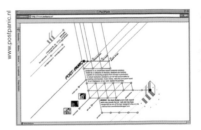

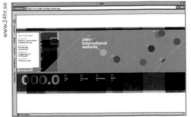

Helvetica is the ultimate typeface; it makes work look anonymous. That's why I hesitated to use it for so long. But I've finally given in to its appeal and begun to use it. Hideki Nakajima

Helvetica arrived in Australia in 1964 – on Letraset. But we welcomed it and we worked with it fervently – letter by letter we rubbed it down! Hour after hour, sheet

Helvetica: Faceless. Alan Kitching

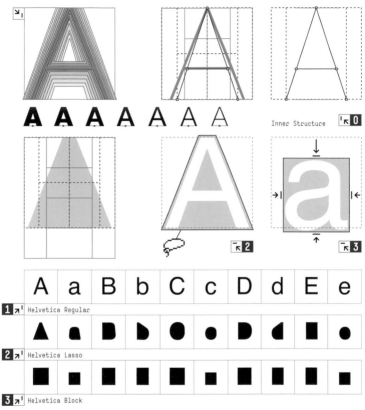

Inner Structure ↖ 0

↖ 2 ↖ 3

A	a	B	b	C	c	D	d	E	e

1 ↗ Helvetica Regular

2 ↗ Helvetica Lasso

3 ↗ Helvetica Block

1 ↗ Despite its drawbacks, the Latin script works; which doesn't speak for its high standards, but for the idea of writing as such – the principle is good, even if it is put to use in a mediocre way. The Latin script is improvised handiwork.

2 ↗ **Despite its drawbacks, the Latin script works; which doesn't speak for its high standards, but for the idea of writing as such – the principle is good, even if it is put to use in a mediocre way. The Latin script is improvised handiwork.**

3 ↗ **Despite its drawbacks, the Latin script works; which doesn't speak for its high standards, but for the idea of writing as such – the principle is good, even if it is put to use in a mediocre way. The Latin script is improvised handiwork.**

Max Kisman, The Netherlands, 1990

Cornel Windlin, Switzerland, 1994

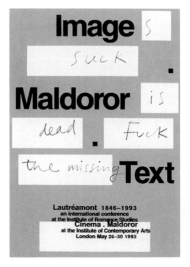

Paul Elliman, United Kingdom, 1993

We hate to like Helvetica. Hamish Muir

Helvetica (a modernist cliche) has been indiscriminately used by the sophisticated, the generic, even the hip. But now it's back, and I feel strangely encouraged. Younger. More vital. Almost... Swiss. Robert Appleton

I howl in pain whenever I see Helvetica misused with the sole agenda of raising the ethical stature of a message. But when it is used naturally, as a default typeface, because of its clarity and LACK of affectation, I feel proud of modern design. Paola Antonelli

FORUM «JUGEND WOHIN?»

VON "ZEBRA" AM TV ENTHUELLT!
ES IST SOWEIT

DIE SVP HÖRT
SOUNDGARDEN

BENUTZEN SIE DESHALB DIE FOLGENDEN PRODUKTE:

24.8. **MELVINS**
&ACETONE

13.10.THE **JON SPENCE R**
BLUES EXPLOSION
&R.L. BURNSIDE &DOO RAG

26.9.**NOMEANSNO**
&ITCH

18.10.**NO FX** &GOOD RIDDANCE
&VANDALS

DIE ROTE FABRIK DANKT FÜR IHR VERSTAENDNIS

ALLE VERANSTALTUNGEN IN DER ROTEN FABRIK, SEESTRASSE 395, 8038 ZÜRICH, BEGINN JEWEILS 21 UHR. VORVERKAUF WIE ÜBLICH.

sehr
sehr
sehr
schlecht

Die 99 schlechtesten Plakate
sind vom 23. November 1994
bis am 15. Januar 1995 im
Museum für Gestaltung Zürich

PRÄMIERT
WEIL
JENSEITS

Säurebad im Mai Sakrale Unterhaltungsmusik
Ralf Brendgens und Michael Gillmeister
Freitag **5.** Mai **12.** Mai **19.** Mai je **20.30** Uhr
Berger Kirche Bergerstrasse **18a**
Labor für Soziale und Ästhetische Entwicklung

Once upon a time, there was a typeface that had the reputation of being more legible and functional than all the others. It was used everywhere and for everything,

Coup. The Netherlands, 2002

31st International Film Festival Rotterdam
January 23 – February 3, 2002

EXPLODING CINEMA

PAUSE

FREEZING MUSIC VIDEO CULTURE.

Homage to a Typeface

I sing the praises of Helvetica, of its forgotten designer[1] and all those who have contributed to its unparalleled international march of triumph over the past forty years. Among them I include amateurs whose work makes a far greater impact on our surroundings than the painstaking efforts of us professionals.

My generation and those since have grown up with Helvetica. It is here to stay. It is so ubiquitous that it is almost invisible. Helvetica is the shift worker and the solo entertainer of typefaces. It is the *conditio sine qua non* of typography. As one among thousands of fonts, it is available but not intrusive. And yet it is one of the most popular in history.

My partiality is inspired by the philosophy embodied in this typeface, its normality and understated self-assurance. Ordinarily, I like having things to choose from. It gives me a feeling of freedom; it is an expression of prosperity. That's why wine lists are long, television channels many, and supermarkets big. I have no objection to that.

When it comes to typefaces I don't need variety.
I remember as a child thinking that all cars
were Volkswagens, that everybody smoked
Gauloise, and that Sunday and chicken
with french fries were inseparable. There was
one television channel and vacations were
always in the same place. I didn't object to that
either.
Helvetica was probably especially widespread
in those days. All I can remember is the great
big orange M of Migros, my family's favorite
supermarket. It looked indescribably modern.
From my later mentors Richard Paul Lohse and
Josef Müller-Brockmann, I learned the rules
and principles of matter-of-fact, functional
design dedicated to content, and the quality
of reduction and restriction. My preference
for Helvetica was not a choice; it was a logical
consequence.[2]

Looking back, one can see that utopian
intentions spurred the development of Swiss
graphic design in the 50s and 60s. The un-
doubtedly modern and useful tools of design
were meant to objectivize the aesthetic

debate; people would make a better choice by means of honest, functional communication. The commercial game rules of this attitude were called information graphics. Akzidenz Grotesk[3] was the typeface of the movement and the sign of recognition among like-minded people. The uniqueness of "Swiss Design" took shape in the design of posters and in corporate design for progressive companies. Success entailed reworking the tools of design, especially the range of typefaces, adapting them to the aesthetic Zeitgeist and to growing functional demands. Around 1957 new Grotesk typefaces came out on the market in rapid succession – Folio, Neue Haas Grotesk, Univers – their appearance more dispassionate and anonymous than that of their predecessor, Akzidenz Grotesk. Adrian Frutiger's Univers was the most independent. Its intelligent system of variations in weight and width, mapped out from the start, later also became the standard for Neue Helvetica. The Swiss Style spread swiftly and many countries adapted it to their own needs. In 1960 Neue Haas Grotesk was renamed Helvetica (Latin for Swiss), a clever marketing ploy, for it ended up becoming synonymous with "Swiss Design." The epitome of understated precision, its attributes appealed to businesses wanting to communicate an incisive and serious identity in their Corporate Design. The prompt adaptation of non-Latin typefaces to the aesthetics of Helvetica and the wide range of language-specific lettering and accents turned Helvetica into the ultimate corporate typeface of the 60s and 70s. However, calling it the typeface of capitalism would miss the mark. If one must mention ideologies, one would have to associate Helvetica more with socialism: accessible to all.

The great leap in technological development and the introduction of the personal computer revolutionized the world of design: it "democratized" the accessibility of design tools. In 1975, at the beginning of my training, my typesetter in Zurich proudly offered "more than 100" typefaces; by 1986 Adobe had already launched a Type Library with 1000 typefaces, including the Neue Helvetica.

The effect on typography was obvious. The appeal of the new technology and supposed liberation from once indispensable basic skills ushered in the fall of the rules governing the classical design of lettering and typography. Since the late 1980s, therefore, the scene has been dominated by rampant growth and stylistic chaos – to every designer his own typeface.

How excitingly old-fashioned, avant-garde and efficient does the conviction seem of those designers capable of solving any problem of design with a handful of typefaces! Helvetica is always among them. This attitude is, of course inseparable from the insight that idea and concept form the basis of intelligent and effective communication. Formalists are vain producers of samples for the software industry and victims of its breathless rat race.

The designs gathered together here in honor of Helvetica have been created by superb designers from all over the world. They could hardly be a more eloquent testimony to the fact that if you have something to say, you will say it even better with this typeface. Anywhere, anytime, in any medium. Helvetica's robust design feeds equally into daring experiments and down-to-earth placards. Anything written in this typeface wants to be read. It lends its quality to the content of a message. Always neutral and functional, it can readily be grasped and has become the quintessence of modern aesthetics worldwide. Subject to cyclical popularity, it is now enjoying a flourishing renaissance and, in time, it will fade into the background again. But we know it will always be there, as a measure of everything else.

Lars Müller

1 Max Miedinger (1910–1980) trained as a typesetter in Zurich and worked as customer counsellor and typeface sales clerk for the Haas'sche Schriftgiesserei in Basel. In 1956 their director, Eduard Hoffmann, commissioned Miedinger to develop a new sans-serif typeface. From 1957 onwards the Neue Haas Grotesk was introduced in its various versions. In 1960 the typeface changed its name to Helvetica. Max Miedinger lived a quiet life in Zurich until his death in 1980. He was not recognized as the designer of his great invention. He is now honored posthumously as one of the most influential typeface designers of all times.
2 Müller-Brockmann and Lohse consistently used Akzidenz Grotesk. Embracing Helvetica was the least I could do to set myself off.
3 The history of Grotesk typefaces their designers and foundries in the 20th century has yet to be fully documented. The relationships between the foundries were close, questions of ownership often confusing. In 1957 the Haas'sche Schriftgiesserei was partially owned by D. Stempel in Frankfurt, which in turn belonged to Linotype. With the advent of digital media, copies of Helvetica proliferated, the most widespread is Arial by Monotype.

New York

PEDESTRIANS →

Cities are the melting pots of visual culture. Open your eyes and explore yours! It is structured and kept alive by a sea of codes and signs, signals and commands. Where there is friction between the ambitions of professional design and the pragmatism of daily problem solving and where the purity of the new merges with the patina of the old, there you will find the visible pulse of the city as the visual complement to street noise and the smell of shish kebab and steaming asphalt. That's what makes you love your city! Discover the charm of the ordinary, the amateur designs by hairdressers and street hawkers: hair raising and ingenious, unabashed and poetic.
Helvetica is the perfume of the city.

L.M.

LOOK RIGHT

LOOK LEF

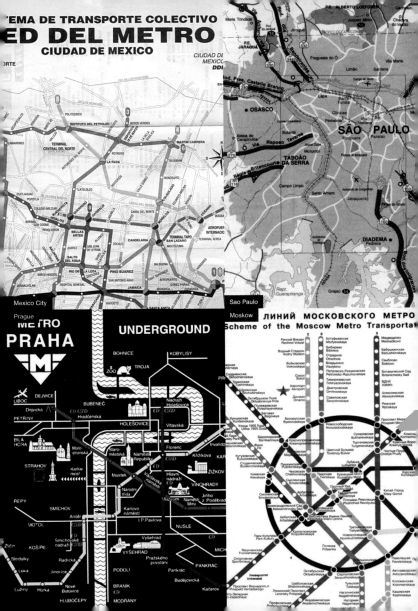

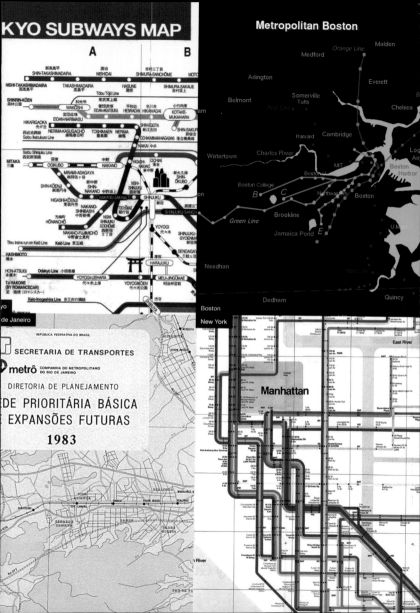

New York

3503

京葉線
Keiyō Line

山手線
Yamanote Line

中央
Chūō L

東海道線
Tōkaidō Line

京浜東北線
Keihin-Tōhoku

Tokyo

Tokyo

Tokyo

10, 12
両編成
4 号車

あさま号
8両編成
2 号車

Uguisudani

47-50 Sts Rockefeller Center Station

B **D** **F** **Q**

New York

8 Street Station

N **R**

owntown platform closed
rom 3/19/01 to 6/25/01

or downtown N R cross Bway &
ake uptown N R to 14 St for
owntown service. Or walk to
stor Pl & Lafayette St & take
train to Canal St for N R service.

U
STADTBAHN
Engelboldstraße
Tarifzone 22
U 1 Vaihingen

ew York

Stuttgart

enna

Dr.-Ka

U3   U4   U1   U2   U6   U3

7

Milano

Tiruvanandapurham

ഫ്പ്പടൽ   प्रस्थान

TILIZZO CORRETTO DEL CARRELLO
HOW TO USE THE TROLLEY

ES   NO

SPORRE IL BAGAGLIO   NON SOVRACCARICARE
PUT LUGGAGE   *DON'T OVERLOAD*

Bagagli da / Luggage from

	LX3604	ZURICH
swissair	SR604	ZURICH
Alitalia	AZ501	BUCHAREST
	RO407	BUCHAREST

PARTURE

A B C D E F

M N O P Q R

Y Z 1 2 3 4

a b c d e f

m n o p q r

y z (. , -

[" " » «]

G H I J K L

S T U V W X

5 6 7 8 9 0

g h i j k l

s t u v w x

; : ! ? —)

+ — = $ £ &

ØL

NO

Copenhagen
New York

SI

enze

ris

BU

GOT HAZARDOUS WASTE?

GO TO:
www.sessionnine.com

New York

Donau Express
Der Fluss tanzt

Mahatma
Sa 15. Juli 2000
19:00 - 04:00

mit Freigelände
Swimmingpool
3 Floors

Ulm

Headliners:02

Mixed by
Sister Bliss

Released 07.05.01

London

SAVE YOURSELF

DON'T HAVE S

London

d e e p

Zurich

sexnight

Liquid

Zurich

licht&liebe / lovenation

Porno-Stars: Dalila &
Manila Mo

Berlin

SLAP & TICKLE PROMO

on lov

IN ASSOC WITH devotion

DRUM & BASS 93
SESSIONS PAR

FRI 25TH
10PM - 6AM
@ BAGLE
YORK WAY, KINGS CROS

ADV.TICKETS £10 M

London

CERNOBYL
HIROSHIMA
MAI PIU'

26 APRILE 11 ANNIVERSARIO DI
CERNOBYL

DA CAORSO A S.DAMIANO

VIA SUBITO LE CENTRALI
E TESTATE NUCLEARI
LL'ITALIA

Bologna

Stockholm

Pd

THE ARTFUL DODGER PRESENTS
RE-REWIND
BACK BY PUBLIC DEMAND
14.08.00

THE NEW SINGLE SINCERE

London

Berlin

XXXI
BOPHILE

INCONTR
CON I FRANCO

Bologna

Stockholm

R. KEL
WITH SPECIAL GUESTS
SUNSHINE ANDE
AND SYLEENA JOH

THEATER @
JULY 21 &

ticketmaster
212-307

New York

Zurich

körupplevelse i globen:

jonas gardell
nilsson
lena philipsson
rs glenmark
4000 körsångare

ests:
peter jöback
te wickman
 c ericson

RAUS AUS DER SCHEISSE...
REIN IN DEN ROCK!

LIVE: DAS DEPARTMENT
DIE GOLDENEN ZITRONEN
FETTES BROT BEATSTEAKS

30. APRIL
O-PLATZ

MACHT VERRÜCKT, WAS EUCH...
...VERRÜCKT MACHT!

williams
Presented in association with
EPSON

MUND
GRU

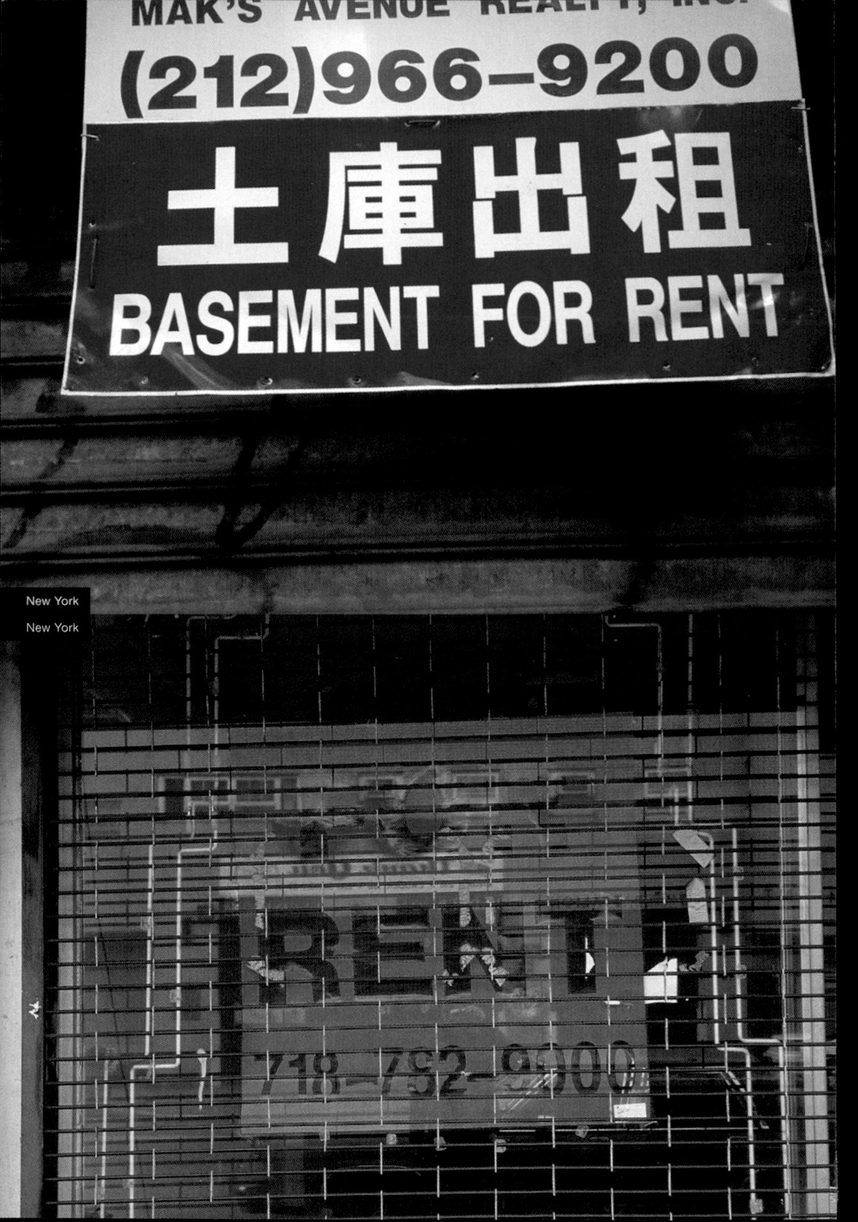

New York

New York

New York

New York

Cairo

Palermo

New York

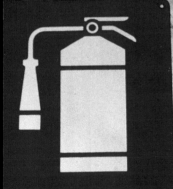

ESTINTORE

N. 2 - 3

EVERY FRIDAY & SATURDAY
BRITAIN'S BIGGEST GAY CLUB
SATURDAY 19 MAY
SCARY SPICE COMES TO GAY
TO LAUNCH HER NEW SINGLE LULLABY
MELANIE B
STEPS
SAT 26 MAY

DOO

London

London

I STAAT WITH A KISS

OPEN

CLOSED

Please Come Again

London

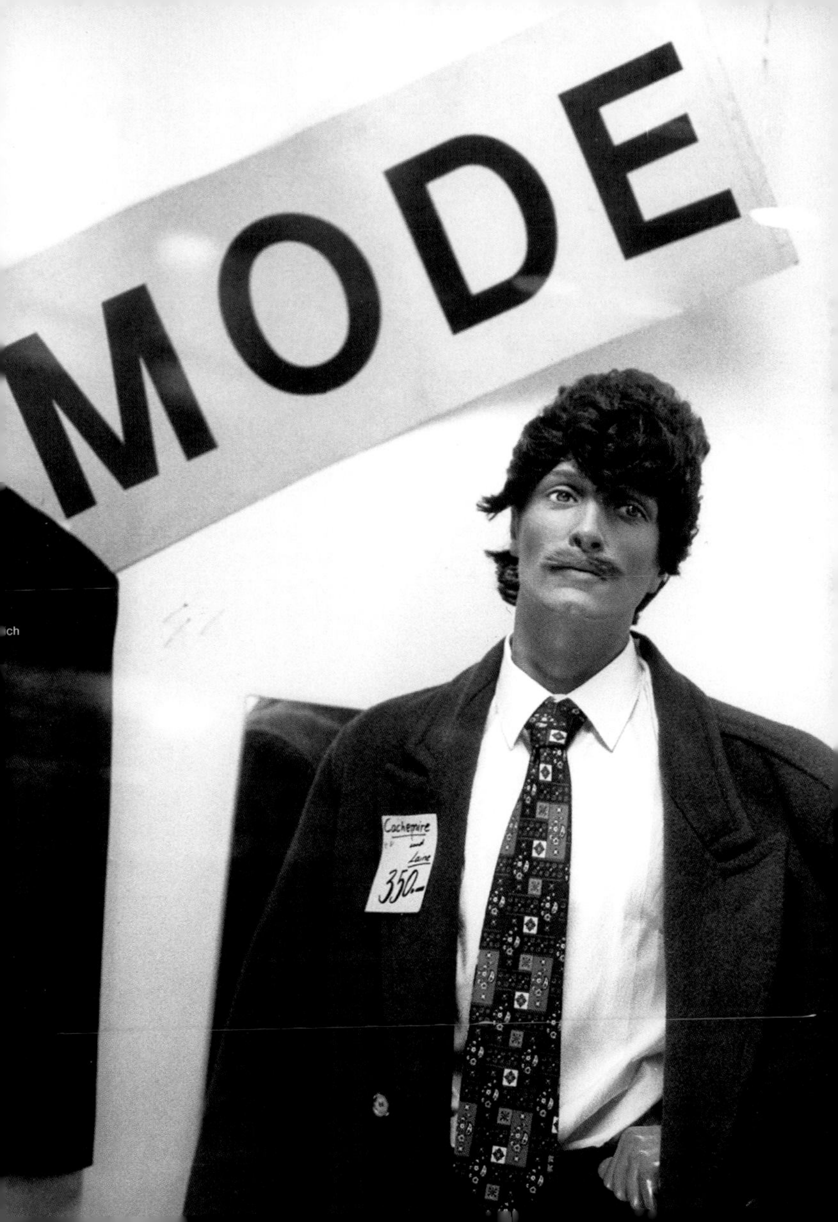
MODE
Cachemire
Laine
350.–

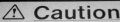

**ATTENZIONE
AI CARICHI
SOSPESI**

Milano

**LAVORI
IN CORSO**

ma

w York

**ATTENZIONE!
PAVIMENTO BAGNATO**

**TAKE CARE!
WET FLOOR**

Milano

Älgar på väg

Stockholm

London

**LAVORI
IN
CORSO**

Bologna

▲CAUTION

**Stand clear
while panel
is in motion.**

▲CAU

**Stop E
and Re
Ignition
Before
ing B**

**DANGER
CONTRACTORS
WORKING
OVERHEAD**

SUPPLIED BY GILROY PLANT

AAAA   A   AAA AAAA   BB,;
   B B C   CCCCCC C   DDD;;
      DD   EEE;
                                   GGG;

GGGGGG   HH   HHHHHHH II
 IIIIII   IIII   JJJ   LLLLLLL;
   LL L   MMMMNNNNN;;
                    N   NNNOOO;;
  OOOOO   OOOOOO   O PPPPP;
    P QQQQQQ   R R RRR
         SSS   SSSSSSSSSS;;
      T   TT T   TTTTTTTU
  UUUU UU U   VVVVVVVW,,
WWWWWW   XXXXYYYYYYYY ZZZZZZZ

  aààáa   a   a aaa   aaaaabbb;
  bbbb   cccccccc cc   d   ddddddd
            éeeeeeeeee   eeeeeee
              e   ffffffffgggg;
ggggg   hhhhhhhhhhhhhhhhhiii;
 iiiiiii   ii i jjjjjjj kkkkk   llllllll
  ll mmmmmmmmmmmm   nnnnnn;;
                         öööööoooo
   oooo ooo   ppppppp
qqqqqqqq   rrr   rrrrrrr   ssss
  ssssssss sss ss   ttttttttttttttttt
 tt üüuüû ûuu   u uuuuuuuvvvvvvv;
wwwwwwwwwwxxxx y yyyyyy zzzzzzzz
   222 333   55   66 7777 8
 89999   000&&????!!ßß££$$;=«»==;;

NATTVARDS MÄSSA | 12

Stockholm
Copenhagen 

LUKKET
SØNDAG

enhagen
ch

New York

The Lamb's   MANHATTAN CHURCH OF THE NAZARENE

BELA

STARS★SHINE
ON
BROADWAY
★SHOE★REPAIR★
WHILE U WAIT
FULL, HALF SOLE
S 20 MIN ZIPPERS
REPAIR
HAND
BAGS
DYE STRETCH

TÄGLICH

OFENFRISCHE

BRÖTCHEN

ELEGTE BRÖTCHEN

ANKAUF

BRIEFE +
RIEFMARKEN
LBER + GOLD
MÜNZEN +
ICHTSKARTEN

kfurt
don

Frankfurt
New York

KEYS
CUT

FORD
NISSAN VW
BMW ETC.
SECURITY
LOCKS

MANICURE
$ 6

X
i
N
G

MANDARIN RESTAURANT 文

RESTAURANT FISCHSTU

London

Zurich

SORRENTO
RESTAURANT-CAFE

CAFFÉ SORRENTO

PIZZA RUSTICA

New York

Roma

Milano

SANDWICH BAR

CAPPUCCINO   TREATS   SANDWI

London

Copenhagen

DINNER SERVICE
JYDEN SMØRREBRØD
31 24 14 28

125

Jyden

Dinner Service

ttino

TRATTORIA FORNO A MATTONI PIZZERIA

RDOGAN MARKET
AMMEL + KALB + RIND
FLEISCH

rankfurt

JEFFERSON
MARKET
TEL:JEF-FERS

New York

OOD CENTER
ZARELLA & SALADS | HOT ITALIAN SPECIALTIES | LATTICINI SOPPRESSATA

FOOD CENTER   186

ew York

ASIATISCHE
LEBENSMITTEL
&
VIDEO

Zurich

bermarkets For Savings

ew York
ndon

SUPER MARKET

146

London
Hamburg

RIF Maroc
Fleisch
Obst · Gemüse

ATLAS MAROC
Frisches Lamm· u. Kalbfleisch (Helal)
Obst u Gemüse · Orient Spezialitäten

Natürliche Haar emacher liche Produkte

Berlin

SALON D.DANZIGER

GABI'S HAARSTUDIO DAMEN ☎7382748

Berlin

Vienna

Frankfurt

London

FRISEURE Petra Catalán

O'Sullivan CONCEPT SALON

SALON de COIFFURE
HOMMES - FEMMES

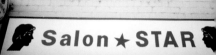

Salon ★ STAR

FRISUR
OTTO FRANZ

FRISEUR

HAIR CUT

HERREFRISØR

FRISØR

energy
BAR

Strike!

THATS NICE

Joker

SUPERIOR
MA

ROMEO

L'ETOILE D'OR

LUXURIANC

20 Kundenparkplätze

Berlin

ZUM BOOTS VERLEIH

PEDONI A SINISTRA

Milano

八重洲中央口
Yaesu Central Exit
八重洲中央出口
야에스 중앙 출구

Tokyo

POST

LUKAS - KAPELLE

Copenhagen

London

New York

YOU ARE HERE

Way out

ROLLS ROYCE

Berlin

MENS
SUITS
Christian Dior
BILL BLASS
EVAN-PICONE
HUGO BOSS
ungaro
FENDI
FERRE
YVES SAINT LAURENT
AND MANY
MORE ...
LOWEST
PRICES

York

SALE
UP TO
50%

New York

SALD

Berlin

SALE

Zurich

SALE

Cologne

SALE

Zurich
New York

SALDI
DI FINE COLLEZIONI

Roma
Venice

SALE

SALDI

saldi

save up to **25%** storewide
endless possibilities sale

Chicago

S A L D I

SALDI

Milano

*is
da
ld
a di

Torino

Roma

New York

SUPER SALE

SAVE UP TO 70%

Additional 15% OFF

SALDI

– exit only

– exit only

New York

– exit only

– exit only

– exit only
turn left to stop sign

Ashland/63 East 63rd

Midway  Linden

Loop Tour Train

Harlem/Lake Kimball

Ashland/63 East 63rd

Midway  Linden

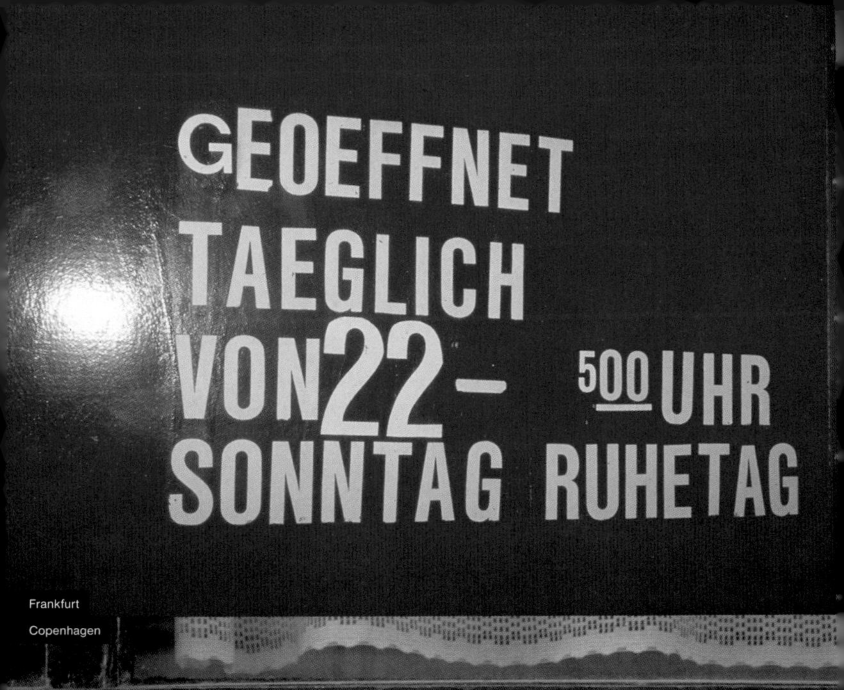

GEOEFFNET
TAEGLICH
VON 22 – 500 UHR
SONNTAG RUHETAG

Frankfurt
Copenhagen

ÅBEN: MAN ~ LØRDAG – 12 - 24
SØNDAG – 17 - 24

Zurich

Helvetia · Platz

EinsteinHaus

York

TRUMP

K A

F E E

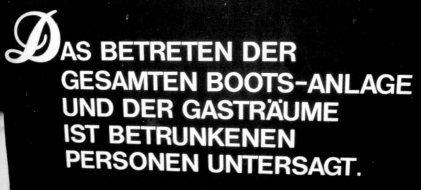

DAS BETRETEN DER
GESAMTEN BOOTS-ANLAGE
UND DER GASTRÄUME
IST BETRUNKENEN
PERSONEN UNTERSAGT.

Frankfurt

San Francisco

Burma

we are not
responsible
for any
damage on
painted rubber
or plastic
bumpers

Notice

All visitors to th
pagoda are requeste
to be properly dresse
   Persons wearir
tank tops mini skirts
or mini shorts are
strictly prohibited.
   Thank you for
your co-operation.
Awwadasariya Sayadaw
   Trustees of
Phaung Daw Oo Pagoc

cannot
accept any
responsibility
for any
removable
radios.

**NO BICYCLES
NO HAND TRUCKS
NO ROLLER BLADES/SKATES**

**ALL DELIVERIES MUST USE
158 CROSBY ST. ELEVATOR**

Roma

Copenhagen

HAS MOVED
TO
259 BOWERY

w York

rich

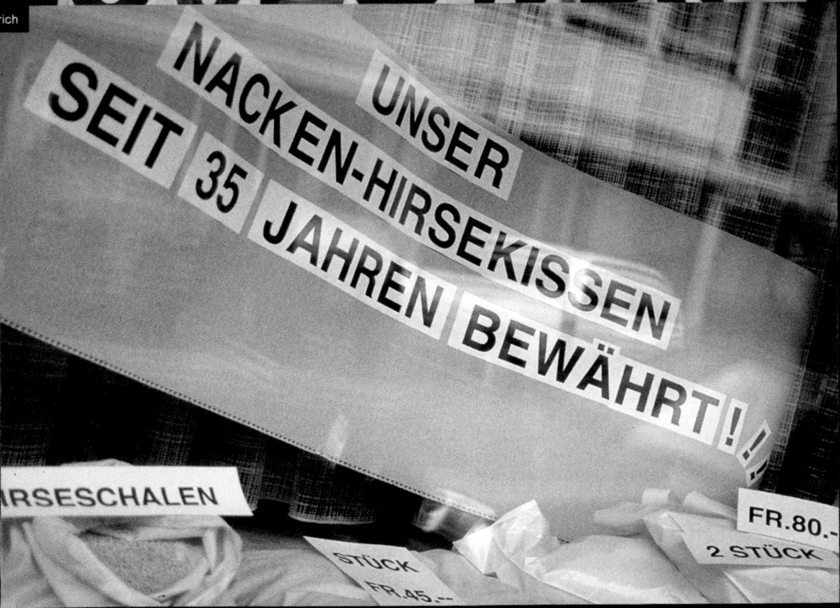
UNSER
NACKEN-HIRSEKISSEN
SEIT 35 JAHREN BEWÄHRT!!
IRSESCHALEN
FR.80.-
2 STÜCK
STÜCK
FR.45.--

Copenhagen

SEKTION **G-H**

G →→

London

Bologna

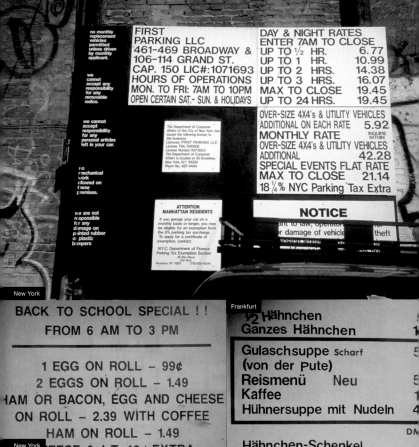

FIRST
PARKING LLC
461-469 BROADWAY &
106-114 GRAND ST.
CAP. 150 LIC#:1071693
HOURS OF OPERATIONS
MON. TO FRI: 7AM TO 10PM
OPEN CERTAIN SAT.- SUN. & HOLIDAYS

no monthly
replacement
vehicles
permitted
unless driven
by monthly
applicant.

we
cannot
accept any
responsibility
for any
removable
radios.

we cannot
accept
responsibility
for any
personal articles
left in your car.

no
mechanical
work
allowed on
these
premises.

we are not
responsible
for any
damage on
printed rubber
or plastic
bumpers.

DAY & NIGHT RATES
ENTER 7AM TO CLOSE
UP TO ½ HR.   6.77
UP TO 1 HR.   10.99
UP TO 2 HRS.   14.38
UP TO 3 HRS.   16.07
MAX TO CLOSE   19.45
UP TO 24 HRS.   19.45

OVER-SIZE 4X4's & UTILITY VEHICLES
ADDITIONAL ON EACH RATE   5.92
MONTHLY RATE   INQUIRE
                       WITHIN
OVER-SIZE 4X4's & UTILITY VEHICLES
ADDITIONAL   42.28
SPECIAL EVENTS FLAT RATE
MAX TO CLOSE   21.14
18 ¼ % NYC Parking Tax Extra

The Department of Consumer
Affairs of the City of New York, has
issued the following license to
this business:
Licenses: FIRST PARKING LLC
License Title: GARAGE
License Number 1071693
The Department of Consumer
Affairs is located at 42 Broadway
New York, N.Y. 10004
Phone No. 487-4444

ATTENTION
MANHATTAN RESIDENTS

If you garage your car on a
monthly basis or longer, you may
be eligble for an exemption from
the 8% parking tax surcharge.
To apply for a certificate of
exemption, contact:

N.Y.C Department of Finance
Parking Tax Exemption Section
25 Elm Place
3rd floor
Brooklyn, NY 11201   (718)935-6044

NOTICE

...ant to law, operato...
...r damage of vehicle...   theft

New York

Frankfurt

BACK TO SCHOOL SPECIAL ! !
FROM 6 AM TO 3 PM

1 EGG ON ROLL – 99¢
2 EGGS ON ROLL – 1.49
HAM OR BACON, EGG AND CHEESE
ON ROLL – 2.39 WITH COFFEE
HAM ON ROLL – 1.49
CHEESE & L.T. 49¢ EXTRA

New York
New York

PEANUTS $1.00
CASHEWS $2.00
ALMONDS $2.00
MIX BAG $2.00
COCONUTS $1.00

½ Hähnchen
Ganzes Hähnchen

Gulaschsuppe Scharf
(von der Pute)
Reismenü   Neu
Kaffee
Hühnersuppe mit Nudeln

Hähnchen-Schenkel
Hähnchen-Flügel
Hähnchenbrust-Filet
Puten-Flügel
Puten-Oberkeule
Puten-Unterkeule
Puten-Schnitzel
Ente
Puten-Frikadelle   St.
Salatteller:- groß
              - klein

AT-CURRY ✳ 4.00
NDSWURST ✳ 3.50
NDS-CURRY ✳ 4.00 DM
OCKWURST 3.50 DM
ENER 3.50 DM
HÄHNCHEN 4.80 DM
MBURGER 4.00 DM
IKADELLEN 3.50 DM
BERKÄSE 3.50 DM
HAS HLIK 4.50 DM
DELSALAT 2.20 DM
ERSALAT 2.20 DM
MATENSALAT 2.20 DM
RKENSALAT 2.20 DM
RTOFFELSALAT 2.20 DM
ÜNE SOSSE .90
ANNKU HEN 2.40
MMES FRIT S
MMES FRIT S, GROSS
AT NBRÖ H N 3.50 DM
EGT BRÖ HEN 2.00 DM
U. WURST 2.00 DM

AUTHORIZED UP
ED/EX SHIPPE
MAIL BOXES
ACKING/SHIPPIN
OSTAL SERVIC
FAX COPIES
LAMINATING
TEL. 782-797
FAX 782-911

New York

換脚色 → MINI PEDICURE
修脚甲 → PEDICURE
修手甲 → MANICURE

NAILS

假甲做膠 → GEL PEDICURE
假甲做粉 → FILL IN
假甲包布 → WRAP

減肥推脂
全身磨砂按摩
BODY SCRUB MASSAGE

中國氣功指壓按摩

☎ :212-966-7487

- 全身按摩　BODY MASSAGE
- 肩頸治療　BACK & NECK TREATMENT TUI-NA
- 減肥推拿　BODY SHAPING ACUPRESSURE
- 中醫指壓　CHINESE ACUPRESSURE
- 脚底按摩　FOOT TUI-NA
- 精巧修甲　MANICURE AND PEDICURE

RADIO

Zurich
New York

Damen

Munich
Chicago

PARK CITY **FLORIST**

New York
Zurich

OTSMTTE →

Frankfurt
Copenhagen

GIFT IDEAS GIFT VOUCHERS

PHOTO STORE

百老匯沖印中心

AFRO

ABSALON HOTEL C TRUM HOTE

New York

Paris

Florence

Milano

Forzano

128 MULBERRY ST.

New York

London

Madrid

Paris

Maiden Lane

112

1540
Broadway
New York

353
353
Zurich

166
New York

CAROLINE 9
Wallis

79MADISON
New York
Palermo

15
Plattenstrasse
New York

22

51 Street

DO NOT ENTER

New York

ziehen

Berlin

drücken

Berlin

Paris

POUR LA VENTE NTREZ PAR LA GAUCHE

Copenhagen

MINI MØNT-VASK Bedst i miles omkreds

Fire exit
keep
clear

IN

DEUR

OPEN

AUTOMATIC
CAUTION
DOOR

SORTIE
DE
VÉHICULES

PRIÈRE DE
NE PAS
STATIONNER

The waiting
is over!

CALL

LOOK
BEFORE
CROSSING

HOT TOPIC

New York

The
September
11th
Fund

To find help or donate
www.september11fund.org

SPACE DONATED BY ARCHIPELAGO

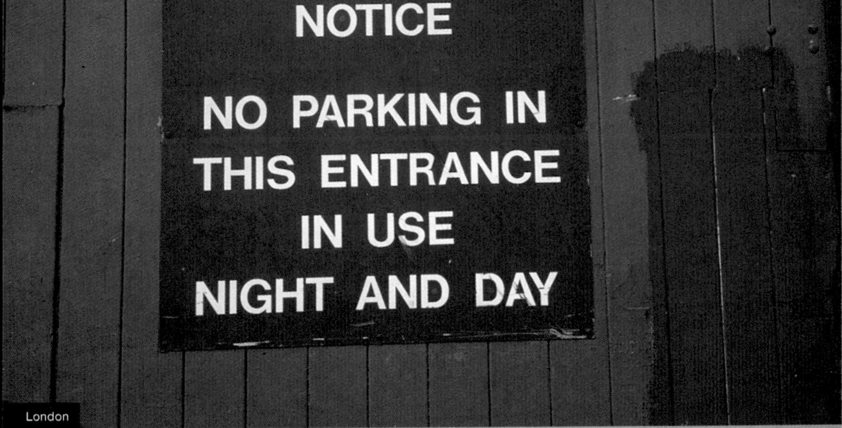

London

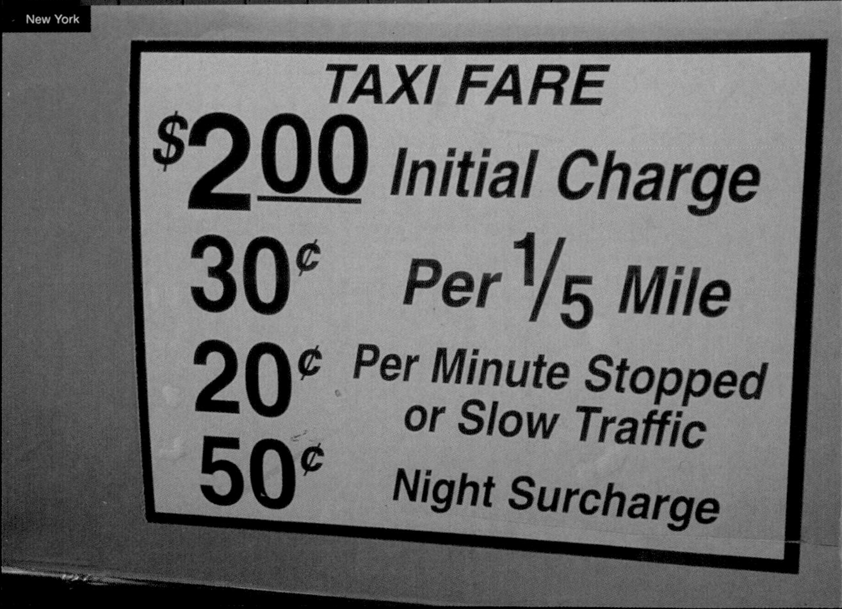

New York

COURIERS,
PLEASE REMOVE YOUR
CRASH HELMETS
WHILST ON THESE
PREMISES.

Thank you.

STALLION
BOOK'S
VIDEO'S

New York

Spain

NO DOGS ALLOWED

PLAYGROUND CLOSES AT DUSK

To report a problem, to learn what we do, or to volunteer

call 1-800-201-PARK

City of New York   Parks & Recreation

www.nycparks.org

New York

Zurich

BRAVO

DOG WASTE
DOG WASTE TRANSMITS DISEASE
CONTAMINATES DRINKING WATER

LEASH–CURB AND CLEAN UP
AFTER YOUR
DOG

IT'S THE LAW!
$25.00 TO $200.00 FINE

IT'S THE LAW

clean up
after
your
dog

maximum
fine $100

public health law

DEPARTMENT OF

New York

New York

ris

Portland

J'AIME
MON QUARTIER

JE RAMASSE

ÈGLEMENT SANITAIRE DÉPARTEMENTAL ART. 99-2
INFRACTION PUNIE PAR UNE AMENDE
POUVANT ATTEINDRE 3000F (457€)

WEYMOUTH AND PORTLAND
BOROUGH COUNCIL

NO DOGS

FROM 1st MAY
UNTIL 30th SEPTEMBER
PLEASE USE AREAS PROVIDED AT
PRESTON BEACH ROAD AND
THE PAVILION END OF BEACH
CHIEF EXECUTIVE

New York

Sevilla

Konstanz

BAIGNADE INTERDITE
SWIMMING PROHIBITED
BADEN VERBOTEN
DIVIETO DI BALNEAZIONE

AUX ABORDS DES ÉPIS

Saint Marie de la Mer
Saint Marie de la Mer

The Hague

SAINTES MARIES DE LA MER

AMIS VACANCIERS

Certaines zones de baignades ne sont pas surveillées,
ou sont interdites.
Des postes de Secours sont à votre disposition.
Veuillez respecter la signalisation et la réglementation.
Flammes indiquées par ces postes
(Crin-Blanc , Arenes , Brise)

▷ **BAIGNADE LIBRE**
▷ **BAIGNADE DANGEREUSE**
▷ **BAIGNADE INTERDITE**

Les chiens et autres animaux sont interdits sur la plage
ainsi que les jets de détritus de toutes sortes.

EN CAS D'URGENCE ☏18

Zuiderstrand

New York

I AM HOLY GHOST INSPIRED

Amsterdam

BUSINESS MARDIFIFI

LAISSEZ·PASSER 2

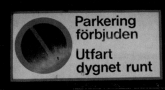

Parkering
förbjuden

Utfart
dygnet runt

Stockholm

zona rimozione

WC

PRIÈRE DE NE PAS STATIONNER

SORTIE DE VOITURES

Chaumont

Amalfi

Leukerbad

NO PARKING
24 HOUR ACTIVE DRIVEWAY

Denver

Dortmund

Einfahrt Tag und
Nacht freihalten

Einfahrt
freihalten!

SORTIE
DE
GARAG

SOSTA
VIETATA

CITY OF WESTMINSTER

NO WAITING
LOADING
UNLOADING

M2293

SUSPENDED
FOR
DIPLOMAT

AUSGENOMMEN
PERSONAL
VEREIN – ALTERSHILFE

EINFAHRT
TAG UND NACHT
FREIHALTEN

PASSO CARRABILE
RIMOZIONE
FORZATA

EINFAHRT FREIHALTEN !

EW YORK'S LARGEST SELECT
OF ART BOOKS

New York

BOOK SHOP

PIRATE BOOK SHO

London
London 

London
Zurich

BOOKS

PAYOT
LIVRES FRANCAIS

books on visual communication and graphic design. The choice of titles is inspired by the publisher's personal and enthusiastic commitment to an area of design that runs a greater risk than most of falling victim to technological euphoria. The series introduces design personalities whose work we think is exemplary – work that might have a chance of slowing down the hurtling train, diminishing the visual noise with comprehensible pictorial language, and underlining the need for creative authorship.

www.lars-muller-publishers.com

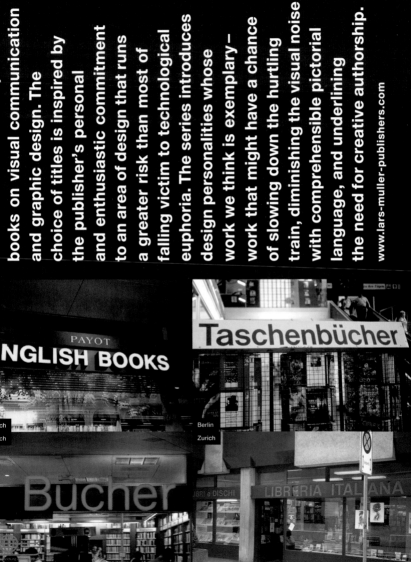

Political Parties in Turkey

Şişli'nin
en önemli
ihtiyacı nedir?

Faziletli
bir belediye
başkanı.

Serdar Yılmaz
Şişli Belediye Başkan Adayı

FAZİLET
PARTİSİ

Beşiktaş'ın
Başkanı var.
Ayfer Atay

CHP

Devletle Milleti
Barıştıracağız!

Hazine, orman
alanları ve vergi
ihtilaflarında
vatandaş lehine
uzlaşma kanunu
çıkacak !

LDP

OYUNUZ BOŞA GİTMESİN!
ANKARA Partilerine verilen
oylar boşa gitmedi mi?

yok!
zm

yağma yok!
Sosyalizm
var

SOSYALİST İKTİDAR PARTİSİ

SİP

SİP

PARANI

SAL

YIKA

yok!
zm

ya
Sos

SOSYAL

New York City Bus

silverlink *metro*

482 219-3
S-Bahn Berlin GmbH

This Bus Uses Clean-A Technology

EMERGENCY EXIT
RELEASE LOCATED
AT BASE OF WINDOW
AT NEXT FORWARD
FACING SEAT

WHEELCHAIR
SECUREMENT

THE WORLD'S

TERS. IOWA

SEVEN CONTIN

STATE FORWAR

OUPS STREETPARADE

Zurich
Zurich 

STAUUNGEN IN DEN BEINEN

HEMERAN!

KINKY

Freezer
Burn
Live
.com

New York
London

New York

New York

Pavement   1962

concrete slabs, cement, shoe prints,
dog excrement, chewing gum.
8000 x 15050 x 10cm

Fragmented mosaic
Comprehensive to road by the same artist.

art you can buy britart.com

New York

BLOO D
DRIVE
TODAY

PLEASE
DONATE

ooklyn/Staten Island
Division o he New York B ood Center

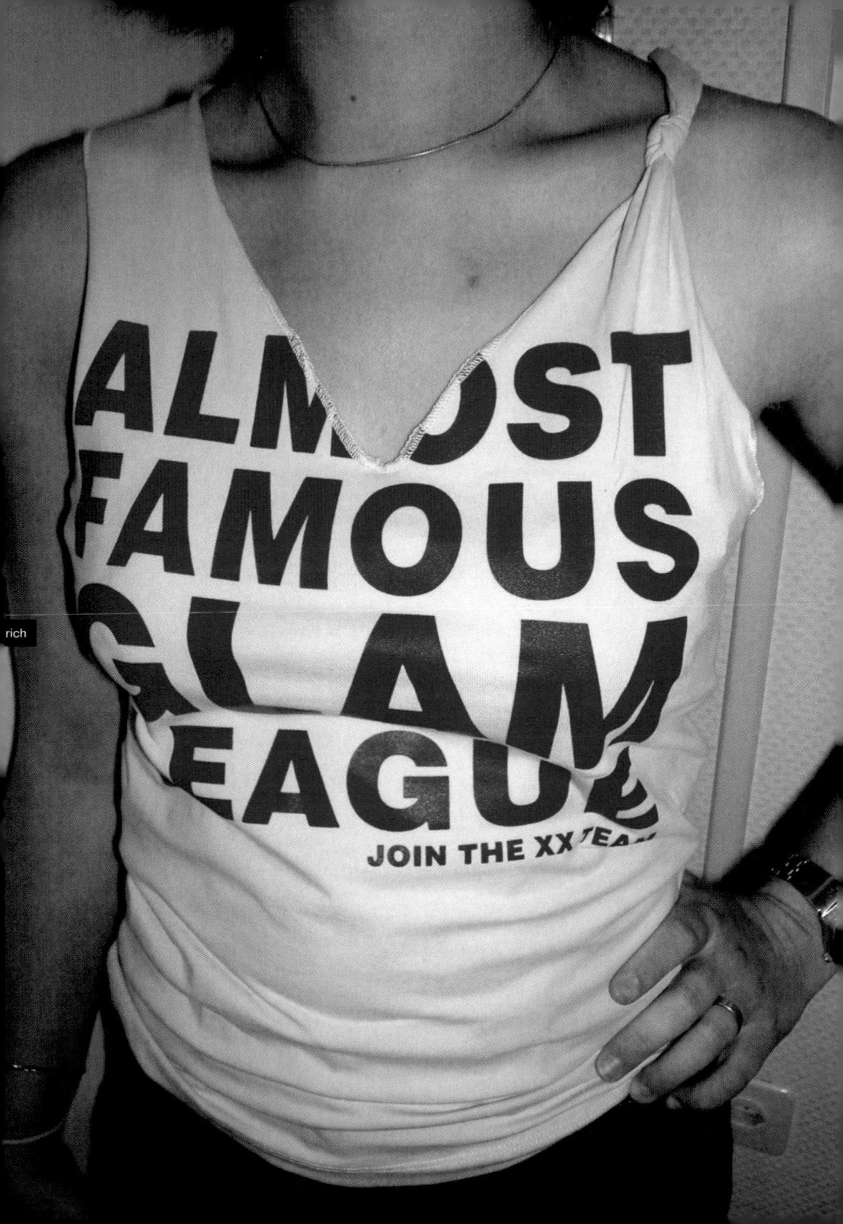

rich

Please No
Littering
Smoking
Spitting
Radio Playing

New York

VIETATO
L'ACCESSO
non addetti
ai lavori

Roma

No
Smokin

London

PASSENGER ENTRANCE ONLY
NO DELIVERIES
EQUIPMENT
HAND TRUCKS
BICYCLES

ALL DELIVERIES MUST
BE MADE AT 166 CROSBY STREET
— NO EXCEPTIONS —

New York

NO PARKING
駐車禁止

Tokyo

TOW-AWAY
NO STOPPING

TIME 7 AM - 4 PM
DATE 1/17 - 1/28

A. Paul CONSTRUCTION
ZONE
FOR TOWED VEHICLES CALL: 415-553-1235

SF ✹ PD
SEC. -22651M C.V.C.

San Francisco

New York

NO SMOKING
Maximum penalty for Smoking
in the seats: £200

London

Not drinking water

Birmingham

Manchester

TRACK
AREA

⊖ **NO ENTRY** ⊖

**Do not enter
or cross
tracks**

34DM

ano | Seattle

NO SMOKING

NO BICYCLE RIDING

City of New York Parks & Recreation

w York

NO ALCOHOLIC BEVERAGES

City of New York ● Parks & Recreation

New York

NO SMOKING

n Diego
ston | New York

NO MECHANICAL WORK PERMITTED ON PREMISES

New York | Denver

O DOGS LLOWED

NO SMOKING

New York ● Parks & Recreation

NO SMOKING

New York

Sonn Farm
Freilandeier + Käse
←
nach 300 m links

Appenzell

VOLKSHEILBAD

Leukerbad

CHAUMONT
PLAN DE VILLE

CENTRE VILLE

RÉIMS
LILLE

TROYES
PARIS

Chaumont

Frankfurt

Bologna

EZIONI UNIVERSITARIE 25-26 MA

MARKEN TEXTILIEN

VOTA
LISTA N.
SINISTRA PE
L'UNIVERSIT

... perché è possibile ritrov
delle idee
e delle ragioni «a sinistra

Per il rinnovo della compo ente studentesca
in seno ai consigl di ammi istrazione dell'Univ
della azienda e GUS

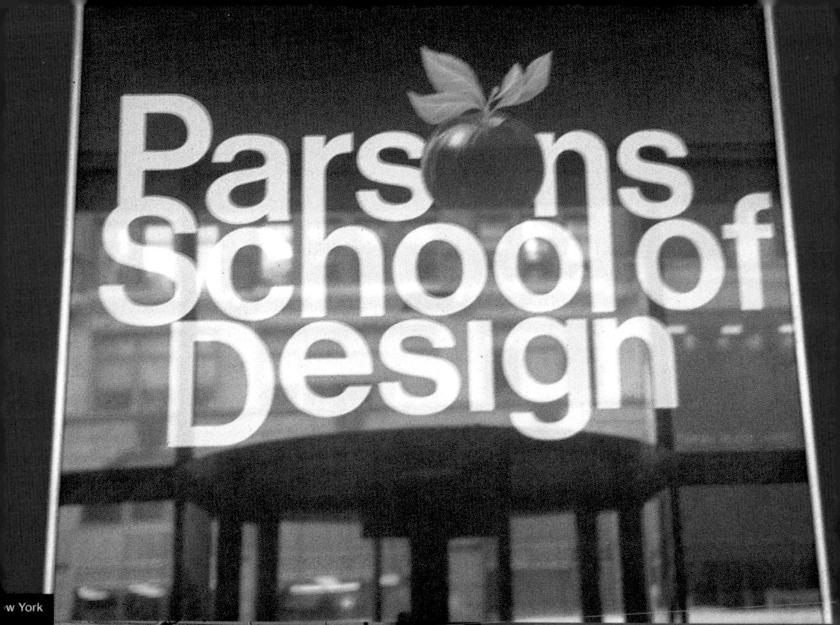

w York

w York

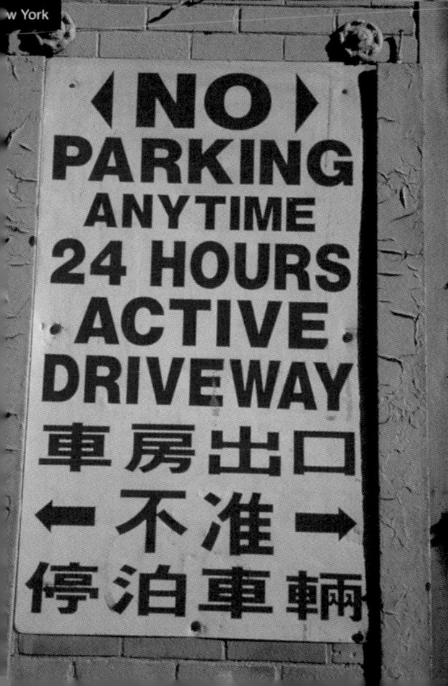

Stockholm

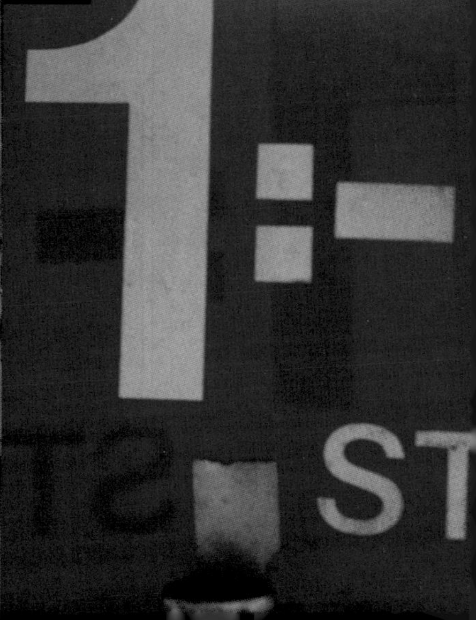

Copenhagen

Chicago

EINWOHNERGEMEINDE

BOLLIGEN

olligen

REALFORM GIRDLE CO

TÄRTOR
SMÖRGÅS
BRÖLLOP
USTA
KASAP

La mostra
delle cartoline
è stata allestita
in memoria
di Lino Bustelli.

Tessin

Stockholm

PS - PC - VERTS - MDC
RADICAUX DE GAUCHE

UNISSONS-NOUS
pour les
PARISIEN(NE)S

Votre PERMANENCE dans

- Candidat aux Elections Européennes 94
- Candidat tête de liste aux Municipales de Paris X° en 95

PS - P
RADIC

UNIS

PA

Hej! Jättemysig etta

Jag önskar byta min etta på Sigtuna
eller 3:a i samma område.
Min lägenhe
köks

Paris

Berlin

WIR
BAUEN UM!

CONGES ANNUELS

FERMETURE
U S 22 JUILLET AU DIMANCHE 20 AOUT

REOUVERTURE

LE LUNDI 21 AOUT

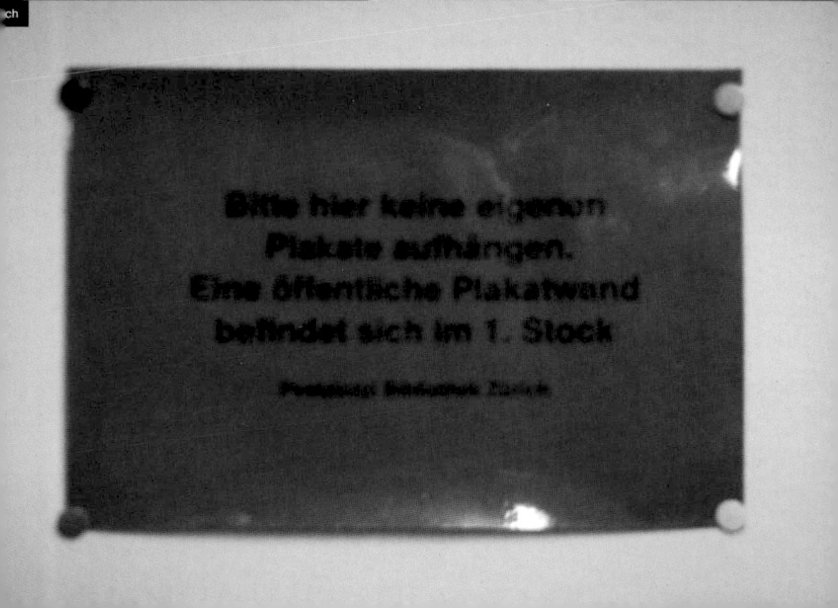

Bitte hier keine eigenen
Plakate aufhängen.
Eine öffentliche Plakatwand
befindet sich im 1. Stock

Pestalozzi Bibliothek Zürich

POL CE LIN

New York
Lucerne

ta gesperrt / sbarr

Our deepest gratitude goes to those from all over the world who responded to our call for contributions to this part of the book. Let the following names stand in for all of them:

Nele Armbruster, Bülent Erkmen, Chiarina Fazio, Steff Geissbühler, Christian Guler, Sonja Haller, Renata Hanselmann, Jan Haux, Melk Imboden, Hitoshi Koizumi, Angela Kreitenweis, Annette Kröger, Hannah Locher, Matthias Megyeri, Lars Müller, Lars Paulsrud, Matilda Plöjel, Markus Reichenbach, Hilda Jvez Salgado, Helmut Schmid, Lukas Schneider, Hendrik Schwantes, Miriam Steymans

The idea for this book arose a few years ago out of a mood and out of the desire to offer an alternative, a constant, to the proliferation of contemporary design. Many of my students and young designers in my studio caught the bug and enthusiastically contributed to the debate and research on this concern. I want to thank all of them, starting with the team that persevered in carrying through on this project and sifting through thousands of pictures to make the selection for this book: Sonja Haller, Matilda Plöjel, and Hendrik Schwantes; and in earlier phases: Nele Armbruster, Jan Haux, Angela Kreitenweis, Renata Hanselmann, Kerstin Ströhlin and special thanks to Timo Kuhn for his irreplaceable contribution to the processing of the pictures.

Most of the professional contributions were placed at our disposal on request. Others, essential to the context of this presentation, have been taken from books. We have done our best to investigate the rights of reproduction. Where this did not succeed, I ask the authors for their understanding and hope that they will delight in finding themselves in such good company. My special thanks go to the Poster Collection of the Museum of Design in Zurich for permission to reproduce their posters.

I also thank my colleagues at Alliance Graphic Internationale AGI and other designers and personalities who responded to our call and spontaneously sent us illuminating and amusing statements on Helvetica.

I thank Friedrich Friedl and Wolfgang Weingart for their professional criticism, and many friends for repeatedly encouraging me to carry this project through.

On the advice of my daughter Hannah, I wish to point out that seven examples of a typeface that is not Helvetica are hidden in this book. My congratulations to those who succeed in the pleasure of discovery.

Lars Müller

schweiz juheee

Some years ago a young intern in our New York office, when looking at an old map where Switzerland was named Helvetia, said, "Fancy naming a country after a typeface." Colin Forbes

Lars Müller
Born in Oslo, Norway in 1955,
Graphic Designer AGI and Publisher.
Lives in Zurich, Switzerland.

Idea and Concept: Lars Müller
Design: Lars Müller, Sonja Haller, Matilda Plöjel, Hendrik Schwantes
Translation: Catherine Schelbert
Pre-Press-Production: Integral Lars Müller
Set in New Helvetica 55/75
Printing: Belvédère Art Books, Oosterbeek, the Netherlands

10th Edition
©2002/2023 Lars Müller Publishers

Lars Müller Publishers
Zurich/Switzerland
www.lars-mueller-publishers.com

Distributed in North America by ARTBOOK | D.A.P.
www.artbook.com

ISBN 978-3-03778-046-6

Printed in the Netherlands